Healed, Restored, Forgiven

Also available from the Canterbury Press

In Sure and Certain Hope
Liturgies, prayers and readings for funerals and memorial services
Written and compiled by Paul Sheppy

A Pastoral Prayer Book
Prayers and readings for times of change, concern and celebration
Raymond Chapman

Healed, Restored, Forgiven

*Liturgies, Prayers and Readings for the
Ministry of Healing*

Written and compiled by
John Gunstone

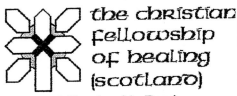

the christian
fellowship
of healing
(scotland)

6 Morningside Road,
EDINBURGH EH10 4DD
Tel: 0131 228 6553

CANTERBURY
PRESS
Norwich

© John Gunstone 2004

First published in 2004 by the Canterbury Press Norwich
(a publishing imprint of Hymns Ancient & Modern Limited,
a registered charity)
St Mary's Works, St Mary's Plain,
Norwich, Norfolk, NR3 3BH

www.scm-canterburypress.co.uk

British Library Cataloguing in Publication data

A catalogue record for this book is available
from the British Library

Scripture quotations are from the New Revised Standard Version
of the Bible, Anglicized Edition, copyright © 1989, 1995 by the
Division of Christian Education of the National Council of the
Churches of Christ in the United States of America, and
are used by permission. All rights reserved.

Quotations from *A Time to Heal* 2000 and *Common Worship* 2000
© Archbishops' Council of the Church of England, and are
used by permission of the publishers, Church House Publishing,
Church House, Great Smith Street, London SW1P 3NZ.

ISBN 1-85311-587-8

Typeset by Regent Typesetting, London
Printed and bound by
Creative Print and Design, Wales

With love to my wife
MARGARET
partner in prayer, ministry and life

CONTENTS

INTRODUCTION

Many churches are developing their healing ministry. Besides the familiar forms of that ministry – intercessions in church, sick Communions, visits to homes and hospitals – there are increasing numbers of public services of prayer with the laying on of hands. Groups of lay persons are being trained to minister to individuals at these services, and also at other times through Christian listening, counselling and inner healing.

It was because of these developments that the bishops of the Church of England commissioned the report, *A Time to Heal*,[1] to survey what was happening, not only among Anglicans but also among other Churches, and to offer guidance and make recommendations concerning the exercise of this ministry. During the same year in which this report was published, *Common Worship* with its services for healing also came into use.

This book is designed to be a companion for clergy and laity involved in these developments. The first five sections contain prayers for individuals facing illness, for groups of intercessors, for prayer ministry teams, and for those preparing to participate, as ministers or as recipients, in healing services.

The following sections contain the text of a service in which prayer with the laying on of hands (and, if appropriate, anointing) is offered, led either by clergy or by lay persons, followed by the same ministry set within the celebration of a Eucharist. In drawing up these services I have had to select from the variety of texts in *Common Worship*. I decided to use only the simpler and more familiar forms of the liturgical prayers, with a minimum number of directions, so that the texts can be adapted easily to any formal or informal situation. The choice of readings, hymns, songs and additional or alternative material is left to those who plan and preside at these celebrations.

The prayers of thanksgiving that follow these services are both for individuals who have received ministry and for teams who have prayed with them. These are followed by a form of the ministry of reconciliation and a collection of prayers for healing from various sources. The final two sections contain texts from the Scriptures and passages from twentieth-century writers on the themes of being healed, restored and forgiven.

I did not think it was appropriate to include prayers for those engaged in the ministry of deliverance. This is a highly sensitive form of ministry and it should not be undertaken without the supervision of those who are experienced and authorized for it. Among Anglicans advice on such cases can be sought from those appointed by a diocesan bishop for that purpose.

I need hardly say that ministry to the sick and troubled does not end with prayers and sacramental signs. It often needs to be followed up with pastoral care which may lead in all sorts of directions, from visiting and co-operating with other care agencies to neighbourly help like doing the shopping and giving lifts to hospital.

We are not usually involved in this ministry for very long before we are confronted with all kinds of opportunities and problems. If I had tried to discuss these, this would have been a very different kind of book. For such matters I recommend the report I have just mentioned. *A Time to Heal*, drawn up by a panel of priests, doctors, hospital chaplains and psychiatrists, is designed as a reference book with guidance and recommendations for most situations in which those who engage in the healing ministry might find themselves.

In this book I have envisaged the exercise of that ministry only in and around the congregation of a local church. The report, however, sees far beyond that limited scene to healing as a 'visionary, prophetic and dynamic' sign of God's kingdom breaking into our suffering and needy world. Like the healing ministry of Jesus Christ, it is an integral part of the gospel he came to proclaim.

'Scholars tell us,' the authors write, 'that in biblical theology there is a close connection between "healing", "salvation" and "wholeness"; and in present-day English "healing" is used to mean anything from recovering from an illness to the complex process whereby individuals, communities and societies are brought into a more harmonious relationship with one another. In other words it involves a fourfold relationship: to the good earth beneath our feet (our physical environment), to other people (our living and human environment), to ourselves (a right ordering of our inner life), and to God (the source of all our being)' (p. 1).

My hope is that this book will encourage many others to share that vision.

PERSONAL PRAYERS

These prayers are for those who are alone, perhaps at home. The first one is the kind of prayer we might want to use when we have a general feeling of being 'out of sorts'. It can be either a passing mood or minor disposition, or it can be a warning of the onset of an illness. If the latter, then we have to make decisions on what we should do. Should we rely on the advice of the pharmacist at the chemist's, or should we make an appointment to see our doctor (1)?

Once the appointment is made, we experience relief that we shall soon have a medical opinion and perhaps treatment, but that is mingled with some apprehension that our condition might be more serious than we thought (2). What is worst about this period of waiting is the uncertainty about our future. We feel we cannot make any definite plans until we know what the diagnosis is. Until we go for our appointment we are shadowed by anxieties which we can only deal with by trusting ourselves to God (3).

Being told we have to go to hospital for further tests and perhaps an operation can be an unpleasant shock, even if we have been half-expecting it. We need to ask for faith that in the ward we will encounter the healing power of Jesus Christ through medical and nursing care (4). Before an operation we may be assailed by doubts and fears – Is it really necessary? – and for those moments we rely on the comfort of the Lord's presence (5).

But sometimes healing does not always come as quickly as we hoped. A long drawn-out illness can shake our faith. Has the Lord heard our prayers? We try to overcome these doubts by daily asking God to reinforce our patience with his love and hope – fruit of the Spirit (6). And if the illness persists and we are warned that we may not get better, then we implore the Lord to hold us up through the waves of bitterness and disappointment until we come to the place where we accept his will for us, whatever that might be (7).

Most of us cherish our independence. We find it difficult when we are compelled to rely on the care of others. The situation can cause tension on both sides, especially when we feel unwell. We need Jesus to be the one who rules us with his compassion and peace (8).

Any breakdown in relationships between people can have an unhealthy effect. If it persists without reconciliation, it becomes a growing dis-ease in us. And if we care about a particular relationship, a breakdown is like a constant pain in our minds and hearts which can result in physical symptoms. We do what we can to resolve the situation by recognizing where we are at fault, and saying sorry to those we have offended and also to God. But if the situation doesn't improve, and if we have done what we can to be reconciled, then we can only commit the matter to God (9).

When healing comes, then we turn to the Lord with thanksgiving, knowing we have been blessed with restored health, not just for our own sake, but so that we are enabled to serve him more faithfully in gratitude for what he has done (10).

We pray with faith because we believe God gives gifts of wholeness to body, mind and spirit. However, we also believe that what he desires most of all is our ever closer relationship with him, which may include a deeper share in the sufferings of Christ.

A Time to Heal

---

1 Unwell

In the day of my trouble I call on you, for you will answer me.

Psalm 86.7

Jesus, my Lord and Saviour,
you know my innermost thoughts and feelings:
grant me your wisdom in the midst of this indisposition.

I do not want to trouble others unnecessarily,
or to be a burden to those who live with me and are nearest to me.
Guide me in what I should do.

Show me anything in my heart or mind
in feelings, thoughts and relationships
which hinders me from receiving your gift of wholeness.
Forgive me and help me to amend anything I can put right.

And may I receive your healing,
not simply for my own comfort and peace of mind,
but so that I may to grow as your faithful servant
to the end of my days.

2 Waiting for an Appointment

Let me hear of your steadfast love in the morning, for in you I put my trust. Teach me the way I should go, for to you I lift up my soul.

Psalm 143.8

Heavenly Father,
I do not know what to expect
as a result of this appointment,
but I believe my times are in your hand.

Thank you for those in the medical profession and their assistants,
especially my doctor,
and enable them to be your agents,
even those among them who do not know
the healing power of your holy name.

Fill those who are to examine me with the Creator Spirit,
so that, through the skills and experience
you have given them,
they may make decisions about me
which are within your will for my life.

I ask this, trusting in the salvation
you have poured upon us
through the ministry, death and resurrection
of your dear Son, my Saviour.

3 Uncertainty

*If I say, 'Surely the darkness shall cover me, and the light around me
become night', even the darkness is not dark to you; the night is as bright
as the day, for darkness is as light to you.*

Psalm 139.11–12

In your wisdom, Father God,
our future is hidden from us,
so that we come to trust in you alone.

I do not know what the outcome of this diagnosis will be,
or how I shall be tomorrow, or the next day;
or what effect it will have on my family and friends.

Part of me longs for the reassurance
that I shall return to full health and strength again.
I shrink from the darkness which looms over the days to come.

But another part of me
– the part that wants to cling to you –
rests in the faith that there is no darkness in the future
where you are sovereign.

May the light of Jesus shine on me
that my doubts and fears may be illuminated
by the glory of his risen life,
and my problem handed over
to your purposes for me.

4   *Healed, Restored, Forgiven*

4 Into Hospital

May grace and peace be yours in abundance in the knowledge of God and of Jesus our Lord.

2 Peter 1.2

Lord Jesus, stay close to me as I go into hospital.

May I experience your presence
and your healing
among the medical and nursing staff.

Guard my heart from unnecessary anxieties and questions,
and strengthen in me the gift of faith,
so that my hope and trust rest solely in you.

Through your grace prepare me
for the daily routine of the ward,
and help me to be a sign of your love
to those around me.

5 Before an Operation

The effect of righteousness will be peace, and the result of righteousness, quietness and trust for ever.

Isaiah 32.17

Righteous Father,
take me into your arms
as I am prepared for this operation
and wheeled into the theatre.

May your love banish my doubts and fears
and defend my mind and heart
with faith and peace.

Guide the surgeons and their staff,
as they attend to me and to other patients
undergoing treatment today.

Let their hands be the hands of Jesus;
and when I return to the ward
fill me with thankfulness for them
and, above all, for you.

6   A Long Illness

*May the God of peace himself sanctify you entirely; and may your spirit
and soul and body be kept sound and blameless at the coming of our Lord
Jesus Christ.*

1 Thessalonians 5.23

Lord Jesus, many prayers have been offered for me.
I ask for your healing every day,
yet still my condition does not improve.
I am tempted, Lord, to ask if you have heard me,
because so often it seems as if you are far away.

But that would be to turn my back on you,
to deny the loving kindness and faithfulness
you have shown me all the days of my life,
and to reject your plans for me.

Forgive me these thoughts and feelings, Lord,
and protect me from them.

I want to kneel in spirit before your cross,
to be united with those saints in every age
who have knelt there and looked into your face.
They offered their pains to you
to share in your great suffering
for my sin and for the sins of the whole world.

In your mercy, fill me with your grace
so that I may be strengthened by your resurrection triumph
and become your disciple among those
who have sought you and still seek you
in the midst of their troubles.

7 Suspected Terminal Illness

*We know that the one who raised the Lord Jesus will raise us also with
Jesus, and will bring us with you into his presence.*

2 Corinthians 4.14

Merciful God,
in your love you raised your Son Jesus Christ
from death by the power of your Holy Spirit.

I praise you for all the love you have shown me
in past days and months and years,
and for the relationships I have enjoyed
with my family and friends,
and with all who have helped and encouraged me.

Anoint me now with the same Spirit,
and cleanse me from my sins
remembered and forgotten.

Through the redeeming grace of Christ's sacrifice,
conquer in me the doubts and fears
of what lies ahead.

Enable me to surrender the rest of my life to your perfect will,
knowing that in Jesus,
and in the company of God's family in heaven and on earth,
I am in your hands now and for all eternity.

8 Carers

A Samaritan while travelling came near the wounded man; and when he saw him, he was moved with pity. He went to him and bandaged his wounds, having poured oil and wine on them. Then he put him on his own animal, brought him to an inn, and took care of him.

Luke 10.33–34

Praise you, Father God,
for those who in many different ways
take care of me during these days.

Banish from me spirits of self-pity, irritation and impatience,
and enable me to find through my carers
your strength in my weakness.

Through your Holy Spirit bestow on them
the grace to assist me as I need;
and through the same Spirit
grant me the grace to receive their care
with gratitude to them and to you.

May I be so conformed to Jesus Christ
in the midst of my weakness
that they may find joy in their service.
Together may we know
we have been in your presence.

9 Relationships

If we walk in the light as he himself is in the light, we have fellowship with one another, and the blood of Jesus his Son cleanses us from all sin.

1 John 1.7

Blessed and glorious Trinity,
Father, Son and Holy Spirit,
perfect unity of love,
I live in a network of relationships
with creation, with people,
with fellow members of the Body of Christ,
and, most wonderfully of all, with you.

I praise you for the life and companionship
which flows to me through them
and in which I find joy and fulfilment.

But some of these relationships are broken or twisted,
leaving me with feelings of regret and disappointment.

Forgive me for what I have done
to cause this situation,
and to deny the power of your love.

By your grace assist me and any I have offended
to recognize our faults,
and to be reconciled to one another and to you.

And for those who cannot yet bring themselves to forgive,
I ask that you will shower them
with the refreshing dew of your love,
and deliver me from feelings of resentment and rejection.

Father, I ask this in the name of Jesus,
who through his cross and the gift of the Spirit,
binds us together in your divine community,
and sends us out into our society
with the gospel of reconciliation for all.

10 Thanksgiving

Then one of the lepers, when he saw that he was healed, turned back, praising God with a loud voice. He prostrated himself at Jesus' feet and thanked him.

Luke 17.15–16

Accept my praise and thanksgiving, merciful and loving Father,
for all the blessings of this life
and especially for the gift of healing
which you have granted me.

Nothing that I am,
and nothing that I have done
made me worthy of such a grace,
yet in your goodness you heard my cry
and saved me through the mediation of Jesus Christ, my Saviour.

Help me to serve you more faithfully
under the banner of his cross,
so that my thankfulness may be expressed
through the way I live
and through my friendships with others.

May I in turn be the disciple of Christ
who helps others to see your gifts
in the healings and other blessings
they receive from you,
and join me thankfully in singing your praise.

PRAYERS FOR INTERCESSORS

Groups meet to pray for the sick in many parishes. Some are linked with societies like the Guild of St Raphael or one of the various Christian centres for healing. The prayers in this chapter are intended for such groups.

A general prayer can include the names of individuals and their situations. We can intercede for them, whatever their illness or trouble, asking that they might be protected from doubts and fears, putting their trust in God (1). Where a known individual is the subject, we can pray more directly for healing unless there are circumstances which require a different kind of prayer (2).

Simplicity is an admirable quality in most prayers, but especially so in the case of children. It is fitting that an intercession for a sick child should be addressed to the Second Person of the Holy Trinity and that reference should be make to the New Testament's model of parenthood in the Virgin Mary and Joseph (3).

Although all the differently abled are not to be classified as ill – indeed, most of them would justifiably assert they are as fit as other people – nevertheless some have to cope with restrictions and frustrations not unlike those faced by the sick. For them healing often takes the form of being better equipped mentally and physically and to live a full and useful life (4). Similarly, old age is not a sickness, but it too brings its own problems. Here, again, healings come through dependence on God, together with appropriate care and physiotherapy (5).

Much of God's healing is mediated through all strands of the health services, even where Jesus Christ is not worshipped or acknowledged. These include places like hospitals (6) and surgeries and health centres (7). A great deal of care is given lovingly and voluntarily by relatives and friends (8). A very special ministry is provided by hospices for the terminally ill (9). How should intercessors pray for the dying? That they might be healed? That they might fall asleep peacefully? Perhaps the best prayer is to offer the individual concerned to the Lord and to trust in his mercy and love (10).

Intercessory prayer, in which we pray individually and corporately for those who are suffering, combines our love with God's love and our will with his will, so as to co-operate with him in building his kingdom.

A Time to Heal

1 General

We always give thanks to God for all of you and mention you in our prayers, constantly remembering before our God and Father your work of faith and labour of love and steadfastness of hope in our Lord Jesus Christ.

1 Thessalonians 1.2–3

Blessed Lord,
we ask you to spread your wings
of loving care and protection
over those who are sick in body, mind or spirit,
especially . . .

Lift them from fear and doubt
with a gift of faith in your healing love,
and draw them closer to Jesus Christ
and the victory of his cross.

Let the wisdom, patience and love of your Holy Spirit
shine through those who attend them,
members of the caring professions,
families and friends.

May they be restored to wholeness
in body, mind and spirit,
and in thanksgiving and praise
glorify your name,
through Jesus Christ our Redeemer and Healer.

2 Individual

Simon's mother-in-law was in bed with a fever, and the disciples told Jesus about her at once. He came and took her by the hand and lifted her up. Then the fever left her, and she began to serve them.

Mark 1.30–31

Lord Jesus, you brought a gift of healing
to the home of Simon Peter,
and when the fever left his wife's mother,
she was able to serve you and your disciples:
come into the home of N in his/her sickness
with that same healing gift.

Take him/her by the hand and lift him/her up
so that, rejoicing in your presence,
he/she may serve you
and your people
in the power of your Holy Spirit.

3 Child

Let your work be manifest to your servants, and your glorious power to their children.

Psalm 90.16

Jesus, good and loving,
you laid your hands on the children and blessed them,
and declared that only like them can we receive
the kingdom of heaven.

Lay your hands on N in his/sickness
and make him/her better.
May he/she know you are his/her Friend and Saviour,
and may those who love this child
rejoice in your goodness.

We offer this prayer
in union with your blessed Mother Mary,
St Joseph and all your saints.

4 Differently Abled

Gracious is the Lord, and righteous; our God is merciful.

Psalm 116.5

Heavenly Father, creator and saviour of all humanity,
we lift our prayers in supplication for all those who suffer
from impediments of sight, hearing, speaking or movement
and for those with mental limitations
which cut them off from easy relationships with those around them.

We pray also for those in the caring professions
who seek to ease the burdens of the differently abled.

Grant to those whose lives are hindered
the courage and determination to overcome
the effects of their condition,
and to those who look after them
patience and understanding.

May they all be led to look to Jesus
who brought healing to the cripples,
the deaf, the blind and the speechless.

And may we learn to be Christ's disciples
in serving those we know
and those we meet.

5 Aged

Young men and women alike, old and young together! Let them praise the name of the Lord, for his name alone is exalted; his glory is above earth and heaven.

Psalm 148.12–13

Lord God, every age is as youth to you;
and every blessing comes fresh
as on the first day of creation.

We praise you for the wisdom and tolerance of the elderly among us,
for all that they have sacrificed and achieved in the past,
and for the graciousness
with which they encourage younger generations.

To those who are physically and mentally incapacitated,
give your renewing strength;
to those who are neglected and lonely
bring surprises of companionship;
to those who are embittered and frightened
offer your consolation and love.

Help us to respect and cherish
those who have been your servants over many years,
to make them feel they are still
valued members of the community.

We ask this in the name of Jesus Christ
who sat among the elders in Jerusalem.

6 Institutional Health Care

O Lord, you are my God; I will exalt you, I will praise your name; for you have done wonderful things, plans formed of old, faithful and sure.

Isaiah 25.1

Father God,
we pray for the hospitals and other institutions
where the sick are treated,
where the troubled are pacified
and where the suicidal are given hope.

We ask that the care exercised by doctors, nurses and others
may reflect your love for all humanity,
and that they in turn may find fulfilment
in what they can do for their patients.

Send your Spirit of reconciliation into places
where rivalry, jealousy and discontent disturb their work,
and grant that justice and peace
may be restored among them.

We intercede for chaplains and Christian visiting teams
in their various ministries to staff and patients.
May they be sensitive messengers of our Saviour,
faithful to their apostolic calling
in carrying out what is required of them.

7 District Health Care

Ever since the creation of the world God's eternal power and divine nature, invisible though they are, have been understood and seen through the things he has made.

Romans 1.20

Lord God of creation,
we pray for doctors, nurses, paramedics and those
whose duties take them into homes and places of work and leisure

where their skills are needed among people.
Be with them in routines and emergencies
that they may become bearers of assurance and healing
to the sick, the distressed and the injured.

We remember particularly ambulance and fire teams
rushed to the scenes of accidents and crimes
where they attend the traumatized,
the wounded and the dying.

Fill them all with your Holy Spirit so that,
knowingly or unknowingly,
they act in the name of him whom you sent
to be your messenger of salvation, Jesus Christ.

8 Relatives and Friends

Truly I tell you, just as you did it to one of the least of these who are
members of my family, you did it to me.

Matthew 25.40

We remember in your presence, Jesus, Servant of God,
those who care for relatives and friends
in their homes and at times of distress:

for daughters and sons looking after aged parents;
for mothers and fathers watching over sick children;
for relatives helping aged members of the family;
for friends who support one another through illness and troubles;
and for those watching in emergency and intensive care wards.

We pray for those who struggle with resentments
because they feel trapped in their situation,
or who suppress anger
because those they care for appear inconsiderate or ungrateful.

Send your strengthening and compassionate Spirit
to help them accept the cost of such caring,
to establish peace and love in their relationships,
and to reward those who care for others by revealing to them
that they are also serving you.

9 Hospices

I am the first and the last, and the living one. I was dead, and see, I am alive for ever and ever.

Revelation 1.17–18

Thank you, risen and reigning Lord Jesus,
for the vision you gave to those who established hospices
where the sick could be cared for
and the dying pass from this life surrounded by those
who through therapy can relieve them of pain
and comfort their fears.

We pray that resources may never be lacking
from statutory and charitable agencies
to support and develop their work,
and that those who serve in them may be rewarded
to see the blessings they bring to others.

May these hospices become places
where you are known as the Saviour
who died and rose again for us
and who is alive for ever more.

10 The Dying

When it was evening on that day, the first day of the week, and the doors
of the house where the disciples had met were locked for fear of the Jews,
Jesus came and stood among them and said, 'Peace be with you.'

John 20.19

Loving and compassionate Father,
your incarnate Son passed out of this life into your glory,
watched by his blessed Mother and the beloved disciple:
hear us as we commend N to your mercy
and remember those who are with him/her at this time.

May your Holy Spirit overshadow and comfort him/her
and prepare him/her for whatever lies before him/her.

We pray that your will may be completed in his/her life
and that there will be rejoicing in heaven
over one whom you have redeemed and made your child.

We ask this in the name of him
who is the resurrection and the life,
our Lord Jesus Christ.

RESPONSIVE PRAYERS

Petitions announced by a leader with responses for the group or congregation (traditionally known as a litany) help everyone participating to feel involved. However, the leader needs to speak with reverence in order to avoid sounding monotonous. Brief silences aid recollection, and names and circumstances can be interjected by others at appropriate places during the prayers.

The first three prayers are general intercessions, the last one longer than the other two. The fourth prayer is addressed to Jesus Christ, recalling accounts of his ministry to the sick related in the Gospels, and the fifth invokes the Holy Spirit on representative members of the caring professions. The final prayer intercedes for various aspects of the Church's healing ministry.

Every person in the congregation is part of this ministry, through private and corporate intercession, in personal prayer, prayer groups and in services. This is a valuable way of reassuring people who do not feel that they have 'special gifts' that they are a precious and valuable part of Jesus Christ's healing ministry.

A Time to Heal

I

We pray for the coming of God's kingdom, saying
Father, by your Spirit
bring in your kingdom.

Send us to bring help to the poor
and freedom to the oppressed:
Father, by your Spirit
bring in your kingdom.

Send us to tell the world
the good news of your healing love:
Father, by your Spirit
bring in your kingdom.

Send us to those who mourn
to bring joy and gladness instead of grief:
Father, by your Spirit
bring in your kingdom.

Send us to proclaim that the time is here
for you to save your people:
Father, by your Spirit
bring in your kingdom.

God of mercy
you know us and love us
and hear our prayer:
keep us in the eternal fellowship
of Jesus Christ our Saviour.
Amen.

Let us bless the Lord.
Thanks be to God.
Blessing, honour and glory be yours,
here and everywhere,
now and for ever.
Amen.

New Patterns for Worship[2]

Responsive Prayers 23

Holy God, in whom we live and move and have our being,
we make our prayer to you, saying,
Lord, hear us.
Lord, graciously hear us.

Grant to all who seek you
the assurance of your presence, your power and your peace.
Lord, hear us.
Lord, graciously hear us.

Grant your healing grace to all who are sick
that they may be made whole in body, mind and spirit.
Lord, hear us.
Lord, graciously hear us.

Grant to all who minister to the suffering
wisdom, skill and patience.
Lord, hear us.
Lord, graciously hear us.

Sustain and support the anxious and fearful
and lift up all who are brought low.
Lord, hear us.
Lord, graciously hear us.

Hear us, Lord of life.
Heal us, and make us whole.

Almighty God,
whose Son revealed in signs and miracles
the wonder of your saving love
renew your people with your heavenly grace
and in all our weakness sustain us by your mighty power;
through Jesus Christ our Lord.
Amen.

Common Worship [3]

3

God the Father, your will for all people is health and salvation.
We praise and bless you, Lord.

God the Son, you came that we might have life,
and might have it more abundantly.
We praise and bless you, Lord.

God the Holy Spirit, you make our bodies the temple of your presence.
We praise and bless you, Lord.

Holy Trinity, one God, in you we live and move and have our being.
We praise and bless you, Lord.

Lord, grant your healing grace to all who are sick, injured or disabled,
that they may be made whole.
Hear us, Lord of life.

Grant to all who are lonely, anxious or depressed
a knowledge of your will and an awareness of your presence.
Hear us, Lord of life.

Grant to all who minister to those who are suffering
wisdom and skill, sympathy and patience.
Hear us, Lord of life.

Mend broken relationships, and restore to those in distress
soundness of mind and serenity of spirit.
Hear us, Lord of life.

Sustain and support those who seek your guidance
and lift up all who are brought low by the trials of this life.
Hear us, Lord of life.

Grant to the dying peace and a holy death,
and uphold by the grace and consolation of your Holy Spirit those
who are bereaved.
Hear us, Lord of life.

Restore to wholeness whatever is broken by human sin,
in our lives, in our nation, and in the world.
Hear us, Lord of life.

You are the Lord who does mighty wonders.
You have declared your power among the peoples.

With you, Lord, is the well of life
and in your light do we see light.

Hear us, Lord of life:
heal us, and make us whole.

We remember especially N and N. . .
Let us pray.

O Lord our God, accept the fervent prayers of your people
in the multitude of your mercies look with compassion
upon us and all who turn to you for help;
for you are gracious, O lover of souls,
and to you we give glory,
Father, Son, and Holy Spirit,
now and for ever.
Amen.

Common Worship[4]

4

Jesus, you raised Peter's mother-in-law from her bed of sickness
and she served you and your disciples:
bring your compassion and healing grace into those homes
where relatives and friends care for the sick,
and may they know the comfort of your presence with them.

Lord, stretch out your hand
and we shall be restored.

Jesus, you gave sight to the blind man,
telling him to go and wash in the pool of Siloam:
look on those who are restricted by disabilities
of sight, hearing, speaking and movement,
that they may be helped to enter into life more fully
and find their healing in the joy of relationships
with you and with those around them.

Lord, stretch out your hand
and we shall be restored.

Jesus, one evening as the sun was setting
you laid hands on many who were sick and healed them:
touch now those who are troubled by mental and emotional
afflictions,
that their burdens may be lifted from them
and that they may find their peace and security in you.

Lord, stretch out your hand
and we shall be restored.

Jesus, you raised to life the son of the widow of Nain,
Lazarus the brother of Martha and Mary,
and the daughter of the ruler of the synagogue,
as prophetic signs of your resurrection:
comfort those who grieve the deaths of those they love,
especially children and young adults,
and kindle in them a new hope in you
as their risen and ascended Lord.

Lord, stretch out your hand
and we shall be restored.

Jesus, you liberated from sin and healed
the paralysed man brought to you by his friends:
have mercy on those who long to be rescued
from addictions which paralyse their lives,
that they may enter the freedom
of the daughters and sons of God.

Lord, stretch out your hand
and we shall be restored.

Jesus, you preached the gospel of the kingdom
and cast out the demons who sought to oppose you:
deliver from evil those who knowingly or innocently
allow demonic influences to infest their lives,
and lead them out of darkness into your glorious light.

Lord, stretch out your hand
and we shall be restored.

Jesus, Lord of life,
accept our prayers and be with us always.
Amen.

(See Mark 1.30–31, John 9.1–7, Mark 1.32–34, John 11.41–44,
Mark 2.1–12, Matt. 12.22–28.)

5

Come, Holy Spirit, glorify Jesus:
come with your wisdom to those
who seek to relieve suffering
and bring healing to the sick and distressed.
We pray:

For medical and nursing teams in hospitals,
from senior to the most junior,
and especially those who are stressed
through overwork or lack of experience.
Hear us, Holy Spirit,
and come with your healing gifts.

For administrators and committees,
for receptionists and for all ancillary staff,
for technicians, caterers and cleaners.
Hear us, Holy Spirit,
and come with your healing gifts.

For psychiatrists and therapists,
restoring minds and bodies and enabling patients to live
at peace with themselves and with their families and friends.
Hear us, Holy Spirit,
and come with your healing gifts.

For ambulance crews and paramedics,
for those receiving the injured into A & E departments,
and for those working in intensive care units.
Hear us, Holy Spirit,
and come with your healing gifts.

For general practitioners
and those employed in local surgeries and clinics,

and for district nurses, midwives and health visitors.
Hear us, Holy Spirit,
and come with your healing gifts.

For those who work in hospices
with the chronically sick and terminally ill,
especially children and young adults.
Hear us, Holy Spirit,
and come with your healing gifts.

For all who work and teach in the universities and colleges
which train doctors, nurses and others in the caring professions.
Hear us, Holy Spirit,
and come with your healing gifts.

For pharmacists and those who develop new therapies,
that right choices may be made for the benefit of all humanity.
Hear us, Holy Spirit,
and come with your healing gifts.

For chaplains and their teams who minister
to staff and patients in the name of Jesus Christ,
and for those of goodwill, and of other faiths,
who have compassion for the sick.
Hear us, Holy Spirit,
and come with your healing gifts.

God our Father
we invoke your Holy Spirit
that his boldness may transform us,
his gentleness may lead us,
and his gifts may equip us
to worship and serve you
in the name of Jesus Christ
now and always.
Amen.

6

Let us praise the Lord for the Church's healing ministry,
pray for those who fulfil it,
and intercede for those who misunderstand it.

We thank you for the gospel proclaimed throughout the Church,
as those who seek your healing and those who pray for them
recognize your saving grace in their lives.
We praise you, Father,
and bless your holy name.

We thank you for your servants in the past
whom you inspired with gifts of faith
to take prophetic initiatives in the healing ministry,
leading the way for us to follow.
We praise you, Father,
and bless your holy name.

We thank you for the responses of the Churches
in providing guidelines and liturgies
to encourage the ministry of healing.
We praise you, Father,
and bless your holy name.

We pray for congregations where the healing ministry is offered,
that you will give strength and wisdom to those who lead,
and faith and prudence to all those involved.
Jesus, come among your people,
and lead us in your way.

We pray for those who train and advise local churches,
communities and groups in the ministry of healing,
that they will faithfully follow the way you lead them.
Jesus, come among your people,
and lead us in your way.

We pray for qualified Christian counsellors,
Christian listeners and Christians in the caring professions,
that they will be filled with the Holy Spirit to minister in your name.

Jesus, come among your people,
and lead us in your way.

We intercede for clergy and congregations
who are fearful of a public ministry of healing,
that you will lead them to others
who can help them discern your will for them.
Spirit of God, guide us
and equip us with your gifts.

We intercede for men, women and children
who have been hurt by false advice or insensitive practices,
that they may they meet others
who will lead them to the Great Physician.
Spirit of God, guide us
and equip us with your gifts.

We intercede for those divided from one another
by differences concerning this ministry,
that they may be reconciled around your Word.
Spirit of God, guide us
and equip us with your gifts.

Father, hear our prayer for the mission of your Church
and make us one in heart and mind
to share the gospel of your kingdom
and to serve you in Christ our Lord.
Amen.

PRAYERS FOR
MINISTRY TEAMS

As I wrote in the introduction, a comparatively recent development in the ministry of healing, at least among Anglicans, is the use of small teams of laity, trained to minister to others during church services and at other times. Members of these teams may also act as visitors to the sick and, if authorized, take them the reserved sacrament.

The charismatic movement, with its stress on the gifts of the Holy Spirit, has been an important factor in this. *A Time to Heal* has much advice on the recruitment, training, activities and supervision of these teams, and the following prayers reflect some of this.

Those invited to join such teams should be Christians who have a sense of calling springing from a lively faith, who are willing to grow spiritually through prayer and teaching, and who are respected by the rest of the congregation (1).

A feature of these teams is that they meet regularly to receive training and to minister to one another (2). Various books and training resources are available for this (most dioceses have an adviser for the healing ministry), but the team will turn to the Scriptures as their inspiration for ministry (3), learning among other things how to discern what is God's will for them (4). It is the normal policy in most teams to minister in pairs; this provides opportunities for training, as the novice can learn from the one with more experience (5).

A distinction needs to be made between qualified and unqualified counsellors. To avoid confusion it is becoming the practice to call the former accredited counsellors and the latter Christian listeners (6).

Occasionally those ministering become aware that a certain case is becoming too complicated for them. They realize there are medical, psychological or spiritual problems which require expert counselling. Referrals are necessary, for example, when there is reason to believe a person may need a ministry of inner healing (7). Because of the sensitive nature of this ministry, proper supervision is vital. Members must be accountable to the leadership, especially in reporting back and following up individual cases while preserving confidentiality (8).

The Gospels tell us that it was compassion which moved our Lord to heal the sick. This is a powerful corrective for any member of a team who may slip into the wrong kind of clinical attitude to those with whom they pray (9). The cornerstone of the healing ministry is prayer – prayer offered in the humility of those who are aware of their own weaknesses but confident in the strength of the Lord (10).

> Many of the gifts within the congregation are given by God to build up the ministry of healing within the Church and to share in its wide range of expression.
>
> *A Time to Heal*

1 New Members

Jesus called the twelve together and gave them power and authority over all demons and to cure diseases, and he sent them out to proclaim the kingdom of God and to heal.

Luke 9.1–2

Heavenly Father,
your Son commissioned his disciples
to preach the gospel of the kingdom
and to heal the sick:
inspire, as at Pentecost, your people today
with those gifts of the Spirit
which enable them
to be living signs of your kingdom.

Help us to recognize those
whom you are equipping by nature and grace
to join us in this ministry,
and prompt them to respond to your call.

So may Jesus Christ continue his healing work
among us and through us with them,
and may your Church become ever more effective
as a being-healed community
bringing your forgiveness and wholeness
to our sick and needy society.

We ask this in his saving name
for your glory.

2 Training

To one is given through the Spirit the utterance of wisdom, and to another the utterance of knowledge according to the same Spirit, to another faith by the same Spirit, to another gifts of healing by the one Spirit.

1 Corinthians 12.8–9

Come to us, Holy Spirit of God,
through the talks we listen to,
the books we read, the discussions we share,
and the events we experience.

Assist us as we seek to learn
more of how to be equipped
to fulfil the mission of the kingdom
among those who are in need of forgiveness,
healing and closer fellowship
with the Father through the Son.

Lead us into your truth and
guide us with your wisdom
so that what we are what we say,
and what we do will be for others
a manifestation in their lives
of the mercy and saving grace of Jesus Christ.

3 The Scriptures

Your word is a lamp to my feet and a light to my path.

Psalm 119.105

Gracious Father,
you have given us the sacred Scriptures
through which you meet with us and talk with us.
In them you have revealed yourself,
your promises and your love.

Send down on us your Holy Spirit
as we reflect on these texts,
and open our hearts as well as our minds
so that through the words of their human authors
we may hear the voice of your Eternal Word.

So may we be transformed in our thinking and feeling
to be faithful messengers of Jesus Christ,
your Word incarnate,
among those who seek your healing grace.

4 Discernment

*Happy are those who find wisdom, and those who get understanding, for
her income is better than silver, and her revenue better than gold.*

Proverbs 3.13–14

Come, Holy Spirit,
enlighten our devotion and understanding
as you enlightened the devotion and understanding
of the Blessed Virgin Mary and of the apostles,
and of Christ's followers in every age.

May your wisdom instruct our minds,
may your love cleanse our hearts,
may your light banish our darkness,
and may your armour defend us from every evil.

Sit us at the feet of the Master,
that with his disciples,
and with all those who heard him speak
and witnessed his miracles,
we may be taught by him in this ministry of the gospel.

So may our lives be pleasing to our heavenly Father,
and faithful to our Saviour, Jesus Christ.

5 Ministering Together

Two are better than one, because they have a good reward for their toil.

Ecclesiastes 4.9

Lord Jesus, you sent your disciples in pairs
to preach the gospel and heal the sick in your name:
give us both the humility and the grace to minister together
to those who come to us for help and prayer.

Enable us through the Holy Spirit
to work in a partnership which fulfils your Word,
that where two or three are gathered in your name,
there you are among them.

Protect us from spirits of competition,
jealousy and confusion,
and from anything that separates us
from you and from one another.

We pray that we may act as one,
united in your Body,
when your Spirit prompts us to intercede for others.
So may the blessings of your kingdom touch them
and lead them in the way you want them to go.

6 Christian Listeners

*And when you turn to the right or when you turn to the left, your ears
shall hear a word behind you, saying, 'This is the way; walk in it.'*

Isaiah 30.21

Loving and merciful Father,
as we meet those who share their troubles with us,
stir up in us the fruit of the Holy Spirit
so that we may see them and listen to them

with the compassion and discernment of Jesus.
Discipline us to be patient with those who exasperate us,
understanding with those who are anxious,
comforting to those who are weak,
accepting with those who feel rejected,
and loving with those who are unattractive.
Above all, guide us when to speak and when to be silent
so as to give them space to express themselves
and opportunities to hear you speaking to them.

May our fellowship with them in the Holy Spirit
lead them to know the presence of Jesus Christ with us,
confirming them in his peace
and filling their hearts with thankfulness to you.

7 Inner Healing

He has sent me to bring good news to the oppressed, to bind up the broken hearted.

Isaiah 61.1

God our Father, you sent Jesus
to bring the gospel to the oppressed
and to bind up the broken hearted:
stay near us as we meet those
whose lives are still oppressed
by memories of personal rejections
and hurtful experiences of past years.

Cover them with the wings of your Spirit
so that in recalling these memories
they discover the light of your presence
in the shadows of their mind.

Send Jesus back with them over those years
and show them the power of his cross and resurrection
to forgive, to heal and to restore them
to closer fellowship with you.

Restrain us from saying or doing anything
which distracts them from that spiritual journey
into wholeness and peace.

Show us when to pray and how to pray with them,
and reveal to them that the love
with which you loved your Son
is in them, and he in them,
as they step forward into a life renewed.

8 Supervision

*Obey your leaders and submit to them, for they are keeping watch over
your souls and will give an account. Let them do this with joy and not
with sighing – for that would be harmful to you.*

Hebrews 13.17

Thank you, Lord God, for those you have called
to preside over our group;
thank you for their love and dedication,
their experience and their insights.

Enable them to discern in the light of the Holy Spirit
the needs and gifts within our team,
and to fulfil your will
as we seek to serve you in this ministry.

Teach us how to support and respect their leadership,
and to learn from their knowledge and experience,
that the ministry we offer will become
a touch of the healing Christ himself,
making us an effective and loving team,
and servants of your kingdom.

9 Compassion

Blessed be the God and Father of our Lord Jesus Christ, the Father of mercies and the God of all consolation, who consoles us in all our affliction, so that we may be able to console those who are in any affliction with the consolation with which we ourselves are consoled by God.

2 Corinthians 1.3–4

Lay your hand upon us, merciful Father,
moment by moment,
while we are beside those who come to us
in sickness or in trouble.

Your compassion for us and for them
was revealed upon the cross,
where your Son suffered for our salvation,
watched by his blessed Mother and his disciple John
who suffered inwardly with him.

May we reach out with your compassion for them,
that they may come to know you are with them
and that you can reach them now
with your love and healing.

10 Intercession

Let us approach the throne of grace with boldness, so that we may receive mercy and find grace to help in time of need.

Hebrews 4.16

Gracious and merciful Father,
we dare to come before you with boldness
for what you have made us
in your dear Son.

We intercede for those who are ill
and in any kind of need.
N and N are in our minds and hearts,
and those who are suffering
and have given up hope.

Breathe upon us,
that our thoughts and words for them
may echo the voice of your Holy Spirit
ascending to your throne,
through Jesus Christ,
our only Saviour and Intercessor.

PRAYERS OF PREPARATION

These are prayers before a service in which a ministry of healing is to be offered. The first five are for individuals seeking ministry; the last five are for the ministry team.

INDIVIDUALS

Joining with God's people in worship can be in itself a healing experience. The words and music of the hymns, the reading of the Scriptures and the faith expressed in the collects and other prayers help us to look away from ourselves and to the Lord's love and promises (1).

We may be shy of putting ourselves forward: What will the rest of the congregation think? Will it undermine my faith if my condition does not improve? These hesitations are understandable. Yet many who overcome them discover a sense of liberation in letting others recognize they have a need. We don't have to pretend any more. Furthermore, most of the congregation will be looking at us with sympathy and praying for us. And it may be that our action will encourage others to seek prayer for themselves (2).

But do I have enough faith to be healed? There are misunderstandings about the role of faith in the healing ministry. Faith for healing isn't the faith we think we should have. Nor is it trust that those who pray with us have an extraordinary healing gift. It is faith in Jesus as our Saviour and Healer. All that is required of us is that, knowing Christ loves us and wants the best for us, we trust in him within the fellowship of his Church (3).

Sometimes we may need healing from psychological or spiritual problems. Then Christian listeners, trained counsellors or spiritual directors may be able to help (4).

We prepare, too, by turning away from ourselves and praying for all those who are going to share in the service, not only the priest, the preacher and the ministry team, but also the rest of the congregation (5).

TEAMS

Those of us who are members of ministry teams meet before a service to discuss the final arrangements and to pray (6). Maybe we feel uneasy before the service begins, like those who are wondering if they should ask for ministry. We are conscious of our failings. We are anxious that we may say or do the wrong thing. But a sense of unworthiness and weakness can make us dependent on the Lord (7). The priest, or the one leading the service, also wants to ask for guidance for the important role of the one who presides; so, too, does the preacher (8 and 9).

Although the prayer for protection is printed last, it is by no means the least important. It may be that things have gone wrong recently – a silly misunderstanding at home just before we came to church, or an incident which made us late. Certainly we should confess any faults to God and seek to amend matters, yet it may also indicate that we are under a spiritual attack. It is not unusual for Christians on a mission for the Lord to find themselves troubled by the devil in this way (10). It may be fitting on certain occasions to keep a simple fast before the service.

> The prayer life of clergy and lay team members is an essential factor in the way in which they can be used in the healing ministry, and its quality is reflected in the way in which they minister and relate to other people.
>
> *A Time to Heal*

INDIVIDUALS

1 Seeking Ministry

Hear my prayer, O Lord; give ear to my supplications in your faithfulness; answer me in your righteousness.

Psalm 143.1

Loving Father,
renew me in faith, hope and love as I prepare
to receive the prayers and ministry of your servants.

Help me to look away from myself and towards you
and towards your Son,
in the power and love of your Holy Spirit.

Deliver me from feelings of self-pity and depression,
and enable me to continue my spiritual pilgrimage
in which I die to myself and rise to new life in Jesus.

May those who pray for me be blessed
by the joy of knowing that they are serving you,
so together we can praise and glorify your name.

2 Hesitations

The fear of others lays a snare, but one who trusts in the Lord is secure.

Proverbs 29.25

Father God, I shrink from revealing my need to others;
they may regard me as a failure,
or as one who does not trust you.
Something inside me holds me back.

Yet in my heart I believe I should ask for prayer,
so fill me with your Holy Spirit
to sweep away these fears.

By his light may I look to Jesus
as he walked among the crowds
healing the sick.

Teach me the humility of Christ,
and may my willingness to receive his grace
through the ministry of his friends
encourage others to come forward,
trusting in your love.
I ask this in his name.

3 Faith

*Jesus said, 'All things can be done for the one who believes.' Immediately
the father of the child (with the unclean spirit) cried out, 'I believe; help
my unbelief!'*

Mark 9.23–24

Jesus, I know that you can heal,
but my faith in you for this
swings from confidence to doubtfulness,
day by day, hour by hour,
even minute by minute.

Then I consider how unworthy I am to approach you.
So many things are wrong in my life –
my relationships, my attitudes, my actions.
Like Paul, I do not do the good I want,
but the evil I do not want is what I do.

I pray that you will grant me the gift of forgiveness
through your victory on Calvary.
May I be cleansed to receive your grace.

May the heavenly Father fill my emptiness with his Spirit
and lift me into the freedom of those
who are the children of his kingdom.

Then may I serve you
with the thankfulness and joy of one
who is being made whole in your name.

4 Inner Healing

*I pray that, according to the riches of his glory, he may grant that you may
be strengthened in your inner being with power through his Spirit, and
that Christ may dwell in your hearts through faith, as you are being
rooted and grounded in love.*

Ephesians 3.16–17

Father God, you knew me, to the very depths of my consciousness,
from the time when I was in my mother's womb,
and every day throughout my life
to this present moment.

You know, too, all the influences
which have made me as I am
– parental, genetic, cultural,
relationships and experiences.

I pray that by your Spirit you will search me out
and reveal to me what there is in my past
which casts shadows on my life today.

In your eternal love, may Jesus Christ
go back over my years and touch with his healing hand
those things which still prevent me from growing
into the wholeness you will for us all.

Heal me and forgive me,
and enable me truly to forgive others,
so that I am able to fulfil
the purposes for which you created and redeemed me.

5 Before the Service

O come, let us worship and bow down, let us kneel before the Lord, our Maker!

Psalm 95.6

In Jesus' name, heavenly Father, I intercede
for all who will be present at this service,
for those who are leading it,
for those who will be ministering,
and for all who will be receiving ministry.

May we lay before his cross
our fears, anxieties and pains,
and see beyond the shadows
the glorious redemption in his resurrection and ascension.

I pray that the Holy Spirit will overshadow me
and all who are present,
that our worship may be an offering of sacrifice and praise
through Jesus Christ.

TEAMS

6 Before the Service

Who shall ascend the hill of the Lord? And who shall stand in his holy place? Those who have clean hands and pure hearts, who do not lift up their souls to what is false, and do not swear deceitfully. They will receive blessing from the Lord, and vindication from the God of their salvation.

Psalm 24.3–5

Be present, Lord Jesus,
as we assemble to worship the Father through you

and minister in your name to those
who seek your healing grace.

Anoint us afresh with your Holy Spirit
to be your servants in this ministry,
as you were the Servant of God among us.

Anoint, too, those who lead this service and those who attend,
and especially those wondering
if they should ask for prayer.
In your love cast away their doubts and fears.

Fill the Church with your Holy Spirit,
revive devotion and hope in us,
and open our ears to hear your Word,
our hearts to receive your grace,
and our lips to praise the Father.

7 Unworthiness

*If we confess our sins, he who is faithful and just will forgive us our sins
and cleanse us from all unrighteousness.*

1 John 1.9

We prepare for this ministry, merciful Father,
knowing we are unworthy to take initiatives in your name.
We are aware of our failings and fears.
We are sinners in need of your forgiveness,
invalids in need of your healing.

But the Scriptures teach
that your people have been chosen
and sanctified by the Spirit
to be obedient to Jesus Christ
and to be sprinkled with his blood.

May our hearts and minds receive the truth that
through your Son's redeeming work on the cross

we are rescued from sin
and filled with the Holy Spirit,
to be ministers of the gospel of the kingdom
for those to whom you send us.

8 The Priest or Leader

You then, my child, be strong in the grace that is in Christ Jesus; and what you have heard from me through many witnesses entrust to faithful people who will be able to teach others as well.

2 Timothy 2.1–2

Heavenly Father, you call and equip your people
to perform different functions in your Church.
I pray that your hand will guide me
as I preside over this celebration,
and that those who exercise ministry during it
may be one with you in the Holy Spirit.

Give me prudence and discernment
so that all may be done, said and sung
according to your ordering,
and reflect your love and compassion.

But, above all, I ask
that through Jesus Christ
and in the power of the Holy Spirit,
our hearts will be lifted in thanksgiving and praise to you
with angels and archangels and all the company of heaven.

9 The Preacher

Let the word of Christ dwell in you richly; teach and admonish one another in all wisdom; and with gratitude in your hearts sing psalms, hymns, and spiritual songs to God.

Colossians 3.16

Come into my mind and heart, Holy Spirit,
and fill me with your wisdom,
so that I may be a faithful messenger and steward
of the Word of God.

Speak to me through the Scriptures,
and may my notes be a guidance, not a bondage.
Shield me from doubts and hesitations
which distort or dilute your truth.

May I so present Christ crucified and risen
as your Great Physician,
that those who hear me will be filled
with the faith, hope, love and joy
which flows from the Father's throne.

10 Protection

Lead me to the rock that is higher than I; for you are my refuge, a
strong tower against the enemy.

Psalm 61.2–3

Almighty and eternal Father,
you sent your Son to vanquish all enemies,
and the Scriptures tell us
that we are more than conquerors
through him who loved us:
protect us from all spiritual evil which may trouble us
as we minister together in Jesus' name.

By the empowering of your Holy Spirit,
arm us against all the attacks of the enemy
in our thoughts, feelings, relationships
and in the unexpected which may confront us.

Under the banner of the cross
and in the power of the same Spirit,

alert us to call on you for our defence,
as the saints have done in every age,
and may we and those with whom we pray
enter into the joy of your triumph.

A SERVICE FOR ANOINTING WITH THE LAYING ON OF HANDS[5]

This is a framework for a healing service to which can be added other readings, testimonies, hymns, songs, psalms and prayers; or the appropriate section of it (5) can be inserted into Morning or Evening Prayer.

I have assumed that the service may be led either by a bishop or priest (President), or by a deacon or lay person (Minister). If led by a Minister, the petitionary form of the absolution in brackets in 4 should be used. The people's texts are printed in **bold**.

A selection of readings for the Ministry of the Word is provided on pages 96–108. For the intercessions, various prayers may be chosen from those found on pages 13–20, 23–31 and 89–93.

If only the laying on of hands with prayer is being offered, the alternative verse in brackets in section 5 may be used.

Experience shows that when significant numbers of a congregation as well as the ministry team have been instructed and learned how to pray expectantly, their corporate presence and faith does much to inspire the healing service and open people's hearts to God's word and grace.

A Time to Heal

1 INTRODUCTION

President/Minister: We have been called out of darkness into God's marvellous light.
Grace and peace be with you.

People: **And also with you.**

The love of God has been poured into our hearts,
through the Holy Spirit who has been given to us:
we dwell in him and he lives in us.
Give thanks to the Lord and call upon his name:
make known his deeds among the peoples.

Sing to God, sing praises to his name:
and speak of all his marvellous works.

Holy, holy, holy, is the Lord God almighty:
who was and is and is to come.

Heavenly Father,
you anointed your Son Jesus Christ
with the Holy Spirit and with power
to bring to us the blessings of your kingdom.
Anoint your Church with the same Holy Spirit,
that we who share in his suffering and victory
may bear witness to the gospel of salvation;
through Jesus Christ, your Son our Lord,
who is alive and reigns with you
in the unity of the Holy Spirit,
one God, now and for ever.
Amen.

2 THE MINISTRY OF THE WORD

Scripture readings

Address

3 Intercessions

Prayers for the Church's ministry of healing and for the sick and troubled

4 An Act of Penitence

The President/Minster introduces the general confession with suitable words.

Lord Jesus, you heal the sick:
Lord have mercy.
Lord have mercy.

Lord Jesus, you forgive sinners:
Christ have mercy.
Christ have mercy.

Lord Jesus, you give yourself to heal us
and bring us strength:
Lord, have mercy.
Lord, have mercy.

God, the Father of mercies,
has reconciled the world to himself
through the death and resurrection of his Son, Jesus Christ,
not holding our sins against us,
but sending his Holy Spirit
to shed abroad his love among us.
By the ministry of reconciliation
entrusted by Christ to his Church,
(*or*, may we) receive his pardon and peace
to stand before him in his strength alone
this day and for ever more.

5 ANOINTING AND LAYING ON OF HANDS

Our help is in the name of the Lord
who has made heaven and earth.
Blessed be the name of the Lord:
now and for ever. Amen.

Blessed are you, sovereign God, gentle and merciful,
creator of heaven and earth.
Your Word brought light out of darkness,
and daily your Spirit renews the face of the earth.
To you be glory and praise for ever.

When we turned away from you in sin,
your anointed Son took our nature and entered our suffering
to bring your healing to those in weakness and distress.
He broke the power of evil and set us free from sin and death
that we might become partakers of his glory.
To you be glory and praise for ever.

His apostles anointed the sick in your name,
bringing wholeness and joy to a broken world.
By your grace renewed each day
you continue the gifts of healing in your Church
that your people may praise your name for ever.
To you be glory and praise for ever.

By the power of your Spirit may your blessing rest
on those who are anointed with this oil in your name
(*or*, on those who receive the laying on of hands);
may they be made whole in body, mind and spirit.
Hear us, good Lord.

Hear the prayer we offer for all your people.
Remember in your mercy those for whom we pray:
heal the sick, raise the fallen, strengthen the faint-hearted
and enfold in your love the fearful and those who have no hope.
Hear us, good Lord.

In the fullness of time complete your gracious work.
Reconcile all things in Christ and make them new,
that we may be restored in your image, renewed in your love,
and serve you as sons and daughters in your kingdom.
Hear us, good Lord.

Through your anointed Son, Jesus Christ, our Lord,
to whom with you and the Holy Spirit
we lift our voices of thanks and praise.

At the laying on of hands

N, in the name of God and trusting in his might alone,
receive Christ's healing touch to make you whole.
May Christ bring you wholeness
of body, mind and spirit,
deliver you from every evil,
and give you his peace.
Amen.

At the anointing

N, I anoint you in the name of God who gives you life.
Receive Christ's forgiveness, his healing and his love.
May the Father of our Lord Jesus Christ
grant you the riches of his grace,
his wholeness and his peace.
Amen.

The almighty Lord,
who is a strong tower for all who put their trust in him,
whom all things in heaven, on earth, and under the earth obey,
be now and ever more your defence.
May you believe and trust that the only name under heaven
given for health and salvation
is the name of our Lord Jesus Christ.
Amen.

6 FINAL PRAYERS

Our Father in heaven
hallowed be your name,
your kingdom come,
your will be done,
on earth as in heaven.
Give us today our daily bread.
Forgive us our sins
as we forgive those who sin against us.
Lead us not into temptation
but deliver us from evil.
For the kingdom, the power, and the glory are yours
now and for ever.
Amen.

God has made us one in Christ.
He has set his seal upon us
and as a pledge of what is to come
has given the Spirit to dwell in our hearts.
And also with you.

Go in the joy and peace of Christ.
Thanks be to God.

ANOINTING AND LAYING ON OF HANDS AT THE EUCHARIST[6]

The texts for this service are those with which most Anglicans will be familiar. In general only the mandatory parts of the *Common Worship* Eucharist are printed so that other readings, testimonies, hymns, songs, psalms and prayers may be added as required.

I have used the word President for the presiding bishop or priest, and Minister for any person, ordained or lay, who shares in the anointing and laying on of hands. The people's texts are printed in **bold**. Members of the congregation may read the lessons and lead the intercessions, according to local custom.

A selection of readings for the Ministry of the Word is provided on pages 96–108. For the intercessions, various prayers may be chosen from those found on pages 13–20, 23–31 and 89–93. An alternative form of the confession is on page 56 and of anointing and laying on of hands on pages 57–58.

Eucharistic Prayer E is printed in full with a special preface, though of course other Eucharistic Prayers may be substituted if preferred.

In the liturgical structure of the Eucharist, the anointing and the laying on of hands is appropriately administered after the act of penitence (a preparation for every kind of healing) and that is where it is printed in the following pages, after the intercessions in section 5. Then the service moves forward to the great act of thanksgiving in the Eucharistic Prayer and Communion. But in practice it is often more convenient to minister the anointing and laying on of hands after the Communion. In this case, the act of penitence in section 6 can either remain where it is, or it can be transferred to the beginning of the service and become part of the Preparation.

When only the laying on of hands with prayer is offered, the alternative verse in brackets in 7 may be used in the prayer *Blessed are you, Sovereign God.*

If the oil for the anointing has not been blessed by a bishop, a short form of blessing is printed at 10 for the President to use at the beginning of 7.

> Where the Word of God is proclaimed and a congregation responds in confession, intercession, praise and sacrament, there is an encounter with the healing Christ.
>
> *A Time to Heal*

1 THE GATHERING

The President:

In the name of Christ we welcome you.
We have been called out of darkness into God's marvellous light.
Grace and peace be with you.

All: **And also with you.**

2 THE PREPARATION

Almighty God,
to whom all hearts are open,
all desires known,
and from whom no secrets are hidden:
cleanse the thoughts of our hearts
by the inspiration of your Holy Spirit,
that we may perfectly love you,
and worthily magnify your holy name;
through Christ our Lord.

The Prayers of Penitence (6) may be said here.

The Collect

Let us pray.

Heavenly Father,
you anointed your Son Jesus Christ
with the Holy Spirit and with power
to bring to us the blessings of your kingdom.
Anoint your Church with the same Holy Spirit,
that we who share in his suffering and victory
may bear witness to the gospel of salvation;
through Jesus Christ, your Son our Lord,
who is alive and reigns with you

in the unity of the Holy Spirit,
one God, now and for ever.
Amen.

3 The Ministry of the Word

*Either one or two readings from the Scriptures precede the Gospel
reading. At the end of each the reader may say:*

This is the word of the Lord.
Thanks be to God.

When the Gospel is announced the reader says:

Hear the Gospel of our Lord Jesus Christ according to N.
Glory to you, O Lord.

At the end:

This is the Gospel of the Lord.
Praise to you, O Christ.

A sermon or instruction may follow.

4 The Affirmation of Faith

Let us declare our faith in God.

**We believe in God the Father
from whom every family
in heaven and on earth is named.**

**We believe in God the Son,
who lives in our hearts through faith,
and fills us with his love.**

We believe in God the Holy Spirit,
who strengthens us with power from on high.

We believe in one God;
Father, Son and Holy Spirit.
Amen.

5 THE PRAYERS OF INTERCESSION

The intercessions may conclude with:

O Lord our God, accept the fervent prayers of your people;
in the multitude of your mercies look with compassion
upon us and all who turn to you for help;
for you are gracious, O lover of souls,
and to you we give glory, Father, Son, and Holy Spirit,
now and for ever.
Amen.

6 THE PRAYERS OF PENITENCE

God shows his love for us
in that while we were still sinners, Christ died for us.
Let us then show our love for him
by confessing our sins in penitence and faith.

Almighty God, our heavenly Father,
we have sinned against you
and against our neighbour
in thought and word and deed,
through negligence, through weakness,
through our own deliberate fault.
We are truly sorry
and repent of all our sins.
For the sake of your Son Jesus Christ,

who died for us,
forgive us all that is past,
and grant that we may serve you in newness of life
to the glory of your name.
Amen.

Almighty God,
who forgives all who truly repent,
have mercy upon you,
pardon and deliver you from all your sins,
confirm and strengthen you in all goodness,
and keep you in life eternal;
through Jesus Christ our Lord.
Amen.

*The Peace is given here if the anointing and the laying on of hands is
not administered until after the Communion.*

7 ANOINTING AND THE LAYING ON OF HANDS

Praise God who made heaven and earth,
who keeps his promise for ever.

Let us give thanks to the Lord our God,
who is worthy of all thanksgiving and praise.

Blessed are you, sovereign God, gentle and merciful,
creator of heaven and earth.
Your Word brought light out of darkness,
and daily your Spirit renews the face of the earth.
Your anointed Son brought healing to those in weakness and distress.
He broke the power of evil and set us free from sin and death
that we might praise your name for ever.
By the power of your Spirit may your blessing rest
on those who are anointed with this oil in your name
(*or*, on those who receive the laying on of hands);

may they be made whole in body, mind and spirit,
restored in your image, renewed in your love,
and serve you as sons and daughters in your kingdom.
Through your anointed Son, Jesus Christ, our Lord,
to whom with you and the Holy Spirit
we lift our voices of thanks and praise.
Blessed be God, our strength and our salvation,
now and for ever.
Amen.

The laying on of hands is administered by the President and/or the
Ministers using these or other suitable words:

In the name of God and trusting in his might alone,
receive Christ's healing touch to make you whole.
May Christ bring you wholeness
of body, mind and spirit,
deliver you from every evil,
and give you his peace.
Amen.

Anointing may be administered by the President and/or the Ministers
using these or other suitable words:

N, I anoint you in the name of God who gives you life.
Receive Christ's forgiveness, his healing and his love.
May the Father of our Lord Jesus Christ
grant you the riches of his grace,
his wholeness and his peace.
Amen.

After the laying on of hands and anointing, the President says:

The almighty Lord,
who is a strong tower for all who put their trust in him,
whom all things in heaven, on earth, and under the earth obey,
be now and ever more your defence.
May you believe and trust that the only name under heaven
given for health and salvation
is the name of our Lord Jesus Christ.
Amen.

8 THE MINISTRY OF THE EUCHARIST

The Peace

God has made us one in Christ.
He has set his seal upon us
and, as a pledge of what is to come,
has given the Spirit to dwell in our hearts.
The peace of the Lord be always with you.
And also with you.

The members of the congregation may be invited by the President to offer one another a sign of peace.

Eucharistic Prayer

The Lord be with you *(or)* The Lord is here.
and also with you.   **His Spirit is with us.**

Lift up your hearts.
We lift them to the Lord.

Let us give thanks to the Lord our God.
It is right to give thanks and praise.

It is right to give you thanks
in sickness and in health,
in suffering and in joy
through Christ our Saviour and Redeemer
who as the Good Samaritan
tends the wounds of body and spirit.
He stands by us and pours out for our healing
the oil of consolation and the wine of renewed hope,
turning the darkness of our pain
into the dawning light of his kingdom.
And so we gladly thank you,
with saints and angels praising you, and *saying*:

Holy, holy, holy Lord,
God of power and might,
heaven and earth are full of your glory.
Hosanna in the highest.
Blessed is he who comes in the name of the Lord.
Hosanna in the highest.

We praise and bless you, loving Father,
through Jesus Christ, our Lord;
and as we obey his command,
send your Holy Spirit,
that broken bread and wine outpoured
may be for us the body and blood of your dear Son.

On the night before he died he had supper with his friends
and, taking bread, he praised you.
He broke the bread, gave it to them and said:
Take, eat; this is my body which is given for you;
do this in remembrance of me.

When supper was ended he took the cup of wine.
Again he praised you, gave it to them and said:
Drink this, all of you;
this is my blood of the new covenant,
which is shed for you and for many for the forgiveness of sins.
Do this, as often as you drink it, in remembrance of me.

So, Father, we remember all that Jesus did,
in him we plead with confidence his sacrifice
made once for all upon the cross.

Bringing before you the bread of life and cup of salvation,
we proclaim his death and resurrection
until he comes in glory.

Great is the mystery of faith:

Christ has died:
Christ is risen:
Christ will come again.

Lord of all life,
help us to work together for that day
when your kingdom comes
and justice and mercy will be seen in all the earth.

Look with favour on your people,
gather us in your loving arms
and bring us with (N *and*) all the saints
to feast at your table in heaven.

Through Christ, and with Christ, and in Christ,
in the unity of the Holy Spirit,
all honour and glory are yours, O loving Father,
for ever and ever.
Amen.

As our Saviour has taught us, so we pray:

**Our Father in heaven,
hallowed be your name,
your kingdom come,
your will be done,
on earth as in heaven.
Give us this day our daily bread.
Forgive us our sins
as we forgive those who sin against us.
Lead us not into temptation
but deliver us from evil.
For the kingdom, the power,
and the glory are yours
now and for ever.
Amen.**

We break this bread
to share in the body of Christ.
**Though we are many, we are one body,
because we all share in one bread.**

Jesus is the Lamb of God
who takes away the sin of the world.
Blessed are those who are called to his supper.

Lord, I am not worthy to receive you,
but only say the word and I shall be healed.

The President, the Ministers and the people receive Communion.

Anointing and the laying on of hands (7) may be administered here.

The Post Communion Prayer

God of all compassion,
by the dying and rising of your Christ
you restore us to yourself
and enfold us in your love.
May we who have been refreshed
with the bread of life and the cup of salvation
be renewed by your healing Spirit
and made ready for the coming of your kingdom;
through Jesus Christ our Lord.
Amen.

9 THE DISMISSAL

May God the holy and undivided Trinity
preserve you in body, mind and spirit,
and bring you safe to that heavenly country
where peace and harmony reign;
and the blessing of God almighty,
the Father, the Son, and the Holy Spirit,
be among you and remain with you always.
Amen.

Go in the peace of Christ.
Thanks be to God.

10 A Short Form of Prayer Over the Oil

The President:

Lord, holy Father, giver of health and salvation,
as your apostles anointed those who were sick and healed them,
so continue the ministry of healing in your Church.
Sanctify this oil, that those who are anointed with it
may be freed from suffering and distress,
find inward peace, and know the joy of your salvation,
through your Son, our Saviour Jesus Christ.
Amen.

PRAYERS OF THANKSGIVING

These are prayers for individuals and for the team to use after a service in which a ministry of healing is to be offered, and at other times.

INDIVIDUALS

Thanksgiving, whatever form it takes, is the most health-giving attitude we can have. The title of the central act of Christian worship – the Eucharist – is a reminder that thanksgiving is at the heart of our discipleship.

Signs of healing are an occasion for such gratitude to God, remembering that we are made whole for his purposes, not just for our comfort (1). Even a step on the way to healing can be a cause of thanksgiving to God and to those who treated us (2). We also thank him for those who pray for us (3).

But when our healing seems to be delayed, our intention to be thankful can be shaken. Instead, we may feel like the Psalmist, who cried out, 'My God, my God, why have you forsaken me?' (Psalm 22.1). Then we recollect that Christ has been here before us, in the dark valley of separation from his Father, and Jesus, the 'wounded healer', seems very close. We pray for perseverance (4) and offer ourselves afresh to his love and mercy (5). Healing can come in different and unexpected ways, but it always begins and ends in drawing near to the Lord. (Questions concerning the results of and follow-up to the ministry of healing are discussed in *A Time to Heal*.)

TEAMS

Praying with others in their need is a privileged experience, and yet it is also a humbling one (6). An important part of our thanksgiving should be a resolution to care afterwards for those we have prayed for, especially those who have been disappointed (7); and to ask the Lord to cover our mistakes (8).

We experience a unique joy when those who have received ministry return to thank God for their recovery and for our prayers (9). That gives us renewed hope for our future ministry together, for which we need the wisdom of the Holy Spirit (10).

The climax, the goal (of the ministry of healing), is not soaring, it is not running, it is walking. For each person, it is carrying on faithfully, no matter what. Occasionally something happens to make the spirit soar like an eagle; now and then someone will get up and run; more often we will see people becoming whole, able to carry on more fully in their everyday lives.

A Time to Heal

INDIVIDUALS

1 Healing

I will bless the Lord at all times; his praise shall continually be in my mouth. My soul makes its boast in the Lord; let the humble hear and be glad.

Psalm 34.1–2

Bless you, Lord Jesus,
for signs of healing.
Thank you for the love you show me
and the freedom I receive through the gift of your Spirit.

Your grace lifts up my heart.
I sing for joy with angels and archangels,
and with the whole company of heaven
at your unending goodness.

Yet I am also humbled
that you should have cared
for such a one as me,
an unworthy member of your holy people.

May my life from today
shine with gratitude to you,
and may I be a sign of your healing and saving grace,
encouraging others to seek you
and to join with me
in praising you precious name.

2 After an Operation

Honour physicians for their services, for the Lord created them; for their gift of healing comes from the Most High.

Ecclesiasticus 38.1–2

Your hands held mine, Lord,
as I underwent this operation.
You also guided the decisions and the hands
of the surgeon and the theatre staff
as they treated me.

Thank you for the gifts of healing
bestowed through medical and nursing care,
especially through those who looked after me.

Thank you, too, for the prayers of family and friends,
and the members of my church,
carrying me through this experience
as on a spiritual stretcher,
and bringing me to this moment of thankfulness.

May I learn to trust you to restore me
in these post-operative days
as I learned to trust you before.

Give me patience to wait,
knowing that my times are in your hands,
and help me to serve you more faithfully
in the purposes of your kingdom.

3 After a Service

We always give thanks to God for all of you and mention you in our prayers, constantly remembering before our God and Father your work of faith and labour of love and steadfastness of hope in our Lord Jesus Christ.

Thessalonians 1.2–3

I came away from that act of worship, loving Father,
with humility, peace and gratitude:
humble because others were willing to pray for me,
at peace because I knew Jesus was close to me,
full of gratitude for the gifts of the Spirit
which through Christ you grant to your people.

Enable me to receive your healing gift in my heart,
and set my mind on things that are above,
not on things that are on earth.

Prompt me each day to recollect,
that, beginning with my baptism,
I have died, and my life is hidden with Christ in you.

Thank you for those who prayed with me and for me,
for their work of faith and labour of love
and steadfastness of hope in our Lord Jesus.

Give them joy in their ministry,
and show me how I can serve you
in response to your blessings in my life.

4 Perseverance

Rejoice always, pray without ceasing, give thanks in all circumstances; for this is the will of God in Christ Jesus for you.

Thessalonians 5.16–18

Lord Jesus, you know the pains and sorrows of this earthly life.
You were despised and rejected,
and nailed on a cross between two thieves.

Be my Intercessor with the Father,
and pray that he may fill me afresh with the Holy Spirit,
that I may have faith, patience and humility
as I wait for your healing hand
to lift me above this affliction.

May the Spirit also kindle in me
a sacred flame of thankfulness in my heart
for your great love,
and for those who love me and pray for me.

I surrender myself to you again as your child,
who died and rose again with you in baptism,
and received the seal of the Spirit
as a foretaste of eternal life.

5 Praise

I appeal to you therefore, brothers and sisters, by the mercies of God, to
present your bodies as a living sacrifice, holy and acceptable to God,
which is your spiritual worship.

Romans 12.1

Thank you, Father God,
for all those with their own troubles and anxieties,
who comfort me as I struggle with my infirmity.

Their example and their prayers inspire me
for I see in them the sincerity of faith in you
which carries them through their affliction
and brings them into the joy of your salvation in your Son.

May I enter more and more
into the Spirit of praise and thanksgiving who upholds them,
and may my body be a sacrifice of praise and thanksgiving,
holy and acceptable to you in Jesus Christ.

PRAYER MINISTRY GROUPS

6 After a Service

I am confident of this, that the one who began a good work among you will bring it to completion by the day of Jesus Christ.

Philippians 1.6

We thank you, God our Father,
for all who worshipped with us,
especially those who asked us
to pray with them in Jesus' name.

Accept what faith, hope and love
they and we were able to offer you.

Meet them in their need,
strengthen them in your love,
confirm them in their hopes,
and build up their faith.

And prompt us if and when they need further help
through prayer and personal care.
So complete the good work you have begun among us
before the day of Jesus Christ.

7 Aftercare

You have granted me life and steadfast love, and your care has preserved my spirit.

Job 10.12

We pray, holy Father,
for any who came to the service
and went away puzzled or disappointed.

They had their own ideas
of what they wanted you to do for them,
and their trust in you may have been shaken
because as yet their hopes have not been fulfilled.

Pour upon them your comforting Spirit.
Show them that even in the midst of such questionings
you are still their loving Father
who saves them through the passion of your Son.

May they draw close to him in the garden of Gethsemane
and from him learn to submit themselves entirely to you,
and guide us in our future ministry with them.
We ask this in Jesus' name.

8 Weakness

Whoever pursues righteousness and kindness will find life and honour.

Proverbs 21.21

We are conscious, Lord,
that not everything in the service was worthy of you.

There were times when the flowing of your Spirit
seemed to be blocked by incidents
which could have been foreseen.

In our listening and praying with people,
we did not always follow
the guidance you were giving us.

We failed you in our lack of trust,
and we failed others in our lack of attention.

We ask that you will pardon us,
and in your sovereignty overrule
the consequences our errors may have had
among those to whom we ministered.

Through the victory of the cross,
sweep aside all evil,
that those who came to you for healing departed rejoicing
in the signs of your kingdom in their lives.

9 Recovery

*It will be said on that day, 'Lo, this is our God; we have waited for him,
so that he might save us. This is the Lord for whom we have waited; let us
be glad and rejoice in his salvation.'*

Isaiah 25.9

We thank you, loving Father,
for those who are realizing each new day
that they are being touched
by the healing grace of your dear Son,
discovering within themselves
a harmony of well-being which they had lost before.

May your Holy Spirit enfold their human gratitude
and transform it into a hymn of thanksgiving for your love,
and for the concern and care
which others have shown them.

We share, too, in their thanksgiving,
grateful that through your gifts
we have a small part in their restoration to wholeness.

Together we pray
that we and they may serve you more faithfully
in the tasks to which you call us,
through Jesus Christ our Lord.

10 Tomorrow

Happy are those whose strength is in you, in whose heart are the highways to Zion.

Psalm 84.5

Jesus Christ, Alpha and Omega,
our beginning and our end,
we thank you for leading us thus far
in your ministry of healing among your people.

We thank you for those who have taught us and encouraged us,
for those who have shared in worship
and in practical service to others,
and for those who have had the faith and humility to ask for our
prayers.

We thank you, too, for our fellowship together as a team
and for the blessings we have received
from you through one another.

Forgive our weaknesses and failures.
Protect any who may have been hurt or misled by our mistakes.
Guard us all from the assaults of the evil one.

Go before us as we seek to follow you in the days ahead.
Endow us with gifts of prophesy and discernment,
so that the ministry of healing in your Church
will be a sign to all of the full gospel which you revealed,
when the Father sent you to save us
through your death, resurrection and ascension,
and the outpouring of the Holy Spirit.

THE MINISTRY OF
RECONCILIATION

The ministry of reconciliation, commonly called making one's confession to a priest, is based on the scriptural truth that when we sin we not only separate ourselves from God but also from fellow members of the Church. Usually we express our penitence by reciting the general confession in the services, with thanksgiving for the forgiveness which is pronounced and a personal resolution to avoid such sins in the future.

But occasionally we are troubled by sins – or, more often, a particular sin – into which we persistently fall. Sometimes we can discuss this fault with a trained counsellor, with whom we can pray for forgiveness. But at other times it may be helpful to make our confession to a priest and to receive the assurance of God's forgiveness through the absolution which he/she pronounces. The priest does this in the name of Jesus Christ and as the representative of the Church from which our sins have separated us.

For those who are unfamiliar with making their confession in this way, here are a few practical notes.

We prepare beforehand by asking God to enlighten our conscience so that we remember our sins (from the last time we went to confession, if we have been before). Some penitents make a list on a piece of paper – to be destroyed afterwards.

We make an appointment to see the priest, or go to church if the times of hearing confessions are advertised. The priest will be sitting in the place where confessions are heard. We go and kneel or sit beside him/her and receive a blessing (1).

A form of making our confession is usually provided like the one printed here, with a space in the text where we mention our sins (2). Or we make our confession in our own words, making sure that we express sorrow for our sins and declare our intention to amend our lives.

The priest may offer some advice, say one or two prayers and then pronounce the absolution (3). With the dismissal (4) we return to our place and quietly thank the Lord for his mercy.

Everything which is said during this ministry of reconciliation is confidential, protected by what is known as the seal of the confessional. The priest is under an obligation never to reveal what has been said, though we are at liberty to approach him/her and discuss our problem further if we wish.

> The ministry of reconciliation, whether or not it is associated with spiritual direction, is in itself an aspect of the healing ministry.
>
> *A Time to Heal*

1

The Penitent:

Bless me, for I have sinned.

The Priest:

The Lord be in your heart and upon your
lips that you may truly and humbly confess your sins,
in the name of the Father, and of the Son,
and of the Holy Spirit.
Amen.

2

The Penitent:

I confess to Almighty God,
to his Church, and to you,
that I have sinned by my own fault
in thought, word, and deed,
in things done and things left undone
(especially since my last confession, which was . . . ago).

The Penitent reads or recites the list of sins, then continues:

For these and for all my others sins
which I cannot now remember,
I am truly sorry.
I pray God to have mercy on me.
I firmly intend amendment of life
and I humbly beg forgiveness of God and his Church,
and I ask you for counsel, direction and absolution.

3

The Priest may offer some words of advice, then continues:

Almighty God have mercy upon you,
forgive all your sins,
and bring you to everlasting life.
Amen.

God, the Father of all mercies,
through his Son Jesus Christ
forgives all who truly repent and believe in him:
by the ministry of reconciliation
which Christ has committed to his Church,
and in the power of the Spirit,
I declare that you are absolved from your sins,
in the name of the Father, and of the Son,
and of the Holy Spirit.
Amen.

Lent, Holy Week, Easter[7]

4

The Priest may add further prayers, and then say:

Depart in peace,
the Lord has put away your sins,
and pray for me, a sinner too.

A SELECTION OF PRAYERS

These texts come from different sources to illustrate the variety of ideas and expectations Christians have in the ministry of healing.

Prayer 1 is a personal prayer, in which we appeal to Jesus with his scriptural titles to different situations and crises our lives (the use of the titles of Jesus is common in prayers of personal devotion, as in hymns and songs); 2 is also personal, but more outward-looking – we draw on our faith in the Lord, and his support in our lives, to intercede for others; 3 takes its language from the Bible to pray for healing.

With 4 we come to a general intercession, expressing the truth that we are healed in order to serve God; 5 is similar, but covers a wider variety of human conditions. In 6 we have an invocation of the Holy Spirit suitable for occasions when we receive ministry from Christian listeners and counsellors.

A more direct appeal for healing is reflected in 7, addressed to the three Persons of the Holy Trinity.

Finally, three prayers from official liturgies: 8 was printed in the Order for the Visitation of the Sick in the *Revised Prayer Book of 1928* and could be used for the laying on of hands if desired; 9 is the prayer for the blessing of oil in the Roman Catholic Church; 10 is used for the same purpose in the Orthodox Church.

References for these prayers are listed in the Sources and Acknowledgements on p. 116.

The healing ministry is one of the greatest opportunities the Church has today for sharing the gospel.

A Time to Heal

1

Jesus,
when I am tempted, be my Shield,
when I fall into sin, be my Saviour,
when I am weak, be my Anointed One,
when I am in pain, be my Physician,
when I am fearful, be my Shepherd,
when I am doubtful, be my Teacher,
when I am spiritually dry, be my Living Water,
when I am confident, be my Master,
when I am struggling, be my Rock,
when I am seeking, be my Way,
when I am in error, be my Truth,
when I am in darkness, be my Light, and
when I draw to my end, be my Coming One.

2

Lord, my support in ministry,
may I be a support for others;
Lord, my strength in times of frailty,
may I be a strength to others;
Lord, my companion in times of loneliness,
may I be a companion to others.
Lord, my light in times of darkness,
may I be a light to others.
Lord, my guide in times of confusion,
may I be a guide to others.
Lord, my rock, my confidence and my joy,
protect me in despair and dismay,
that I may complete my pilgrimage
which began, continues and will end,
with him, in you.

Retired Clergy Association[8]

3

God, heal the dullness of our hearts,
that we may listen and hear,
look and indeed perceive.
Use your power to restore our world.
Let all people know your healing touch.
May the least and the greatest experience your healing.
Bless us always with someone to care.
Send us anew to proclaim your kingdom
with authority and power to heal.
Even when the moment of death draws near,
your healing touch can save.
Open our eyes and soften our hearts,
that understanding and healing will be ours.
Take away, God, our hardness of hearing,
our blindness that cannot see.
Gift us with listening, understanding hearts.
Let us turn to you and be healed.

Praying the Good News[9]

(See Matt. 13.15, Luke 15.17, Luke 7.2,3, Luke 9.2, John 4.46, 47,
John 12.40, Matt. 13.15.)

4

O God the Creator and Father of all,
we praise you that your will is life and health and strength.
Help all who are ill or in pain
to place themselves in your hands in loving trust,
so that your healing life may flow into them
to make them well and strong,
able and ready to do your holy will,
through him who has made known to us
both your love and your will,
even Jesus Christ our Lord.

One Man's Prayers[10]

5

O Holy Spirit who dost delve into all things,
even the deep things of God
and the deep things of man,
we pray thee to penetrate the springs of personality
of all who are sick in mind,
to bring them cleansing, healing, and unity.
Sanctify all memory, dispel all fear,
bring them to love thee
with all their mind and will,
that they may be made
and glorify thee for ever.
We ask this in the name of him
who cast out devils and healed men's minds,
even Jesus Christ our Lord.

One Man's Prayers[10]

6

Most merciful Lord, we ask your blessing
on all those who are sick in mind or body.
Comfort and cheer them that they may have courage and fortitude
to face the pain and suffering laid upon them.
We pray for the physically handicapped, for the deaf, dumb and
blind;
for those who have lost the power of reason
and those whose pain is worse in the slow night hours.
We remember especially those who are terminally ill
and we give thanks for all doctors, nurses, relatives and friends
who, by their devotion and skill,
tend to the needs of those committed to their care.
Finally we pray for all who have to bear suffering of any kind
(*names* . . .)
May they turn to you, Lord, for strength, encourgement and
consolation.

Prayers for Everyday Use[11]

7

In the Name of God most High
may release from thy pain be given thee,
and thy health be restored according to his holy will.
In the Name of Jesus Christ, the Prince of Life,
may new life quicken thy mortal body.
In the Name of the Holy Spirit,
mayest thou receive inward health,
and the peace which passeth all understanding.
And the God of all peace sanctify you wholly:
and may your spirit and soul and body be preserved entire,
without blame at the coming of our Lord Jesus Christ.

The Parson's Handbook[12]

8

O Almighty God, who art the giver of all health,
and the aid of them that seek to thee for succour:
We call upon thee for thy help and
mercifully to be shewed upon this thy servant,
that being healed of *his* infirmities
he may give thanks unto thee in thy holy Church;
through Jesus Christ our Lord.

Revised Prayer Book of 1928

9

God of all consolation,
you chose and sent your Son to heal the world.
Graciously listen to our prayer of faith:
send the power of your Holy Spirit, the Consoler,
into this precious oil, this soothing ointment,
this rich gift, this fruit of the earth.
Bless this oil and sanctify it for our use.

Make this oil a remedy for all who are anointed with it;
heal them in body, in soul, and in spirit,
and deliver them from every affliction.
We ask this through our Lord Jesus Christ, your Son,
who lives and reigns with you and the Holy Spirit,
one God, now and for ever.

10

O Lord, who in your mercy and compassion
heals the disorders of our souls and of our bodies:
do you yourself, O Master, hallow this oil
that it may become a healing remedy for those anointed with it
and may set them free from all suffering,
from all defilement of flesh and spirit,
and from all that is evil:
that so also your all-holy name,
of the Father, and of the Son, and of the Holy Spirit,
may thereby be glorified,
now, and always, and for ever and ever.

(See also the formulas for the blessing of oil on pp. 57–58 and 66–67.)

SOME SUGGESTED BIBLE READINGS

The biblical passages in this chapter can be used as readings in church services and in groups, and also for private meditation and prayer. Along with many other passages not printed here, they tell how God's saving, healing grace was brought into the world through Jesus Christ in the power of the Holy Spirit.

In the Old Testament texts we read how that healing grace was revealed to chroniclers, prophets and psalmists, and how they responded in faith to God. In the Gospel texts we have living pictures of Jesus' ministry exercised in different situations, each showing aspects of the boundless mercy and love of God. And in the rest of the New Testament we are introduced to the activities and teaching of the apostles after Pentecost, when they continued that ministry in the power of the same Spirit who had anointed Jesus.

Through such passages, also, we may discover again and again how the Bible becomes a meeting place where we enter into a dialogue with God – where, as someone once beautifully put it, 'the Bridegroom and the Bride speak together'.

When Jesus was baptized in the waters of the river Jordan (Mark 1.8f.), and the Holy Spirit descended upon him, God inaugurated a ministry of healing that was to change the world.

A Time to Heal

OLD TESTAMENT

2 KINGS 5.9–14 *The Healing of Naaman*

Naaman came with his horses and chariots, and halted at the entrance of Elisha's house. Elisha sent a messenger to him, saying, 'Go, wash in the Jordan seven times, and your flesh shall be restored and you shall be clean.' But Naaman became angry and went away, saying, 'I thought that for me he would surely come out, and stand and call on the name of the Lord his God, and would wave his hand over the spot, and cure the leprosy! Are not Abana and Pharpar, the rivers of Damascus, better than all the waters of Israel? Could I not wash in them, and be clean?' He turned and went away in a rage. But his servants approached and said to him, 'Father, if the prophet had commanded you to do something difficult, would you not have done it? How much more, when all he said to you was, "Wash, and be clean"?' So he went down and immersed himself seven times in the Jordan, according to the word of the man of God; his flesh was restored like the flesh of a young boy, and he was clean.

ISAIAH 55.6–11 *Seek the Lord*

Seek the Lord while he may be found, call upon him while he is near; let the wicked forsake their way, and the unrighteous their thoughts; let them return to the Lord, that he may have mercy on them, and to our God, for he will abundantly pardon. For my thoughts are not your thoughts, nor are your ways my ways, says the Lord. For as the heavens are higher than the earth, so are my ways higher than your ways and my thoughts than your thoughts. For as the rain and the snow come down from heaven, and do not return there until they have watered the earth, making it bring forth and sprout, giving seed to the sower and bread to the eater, so shall my word be that goes out from my mouth; it shall not return to me empty, but it shall accomplish that which I purpose, and succeed in the thing for which I sent it.

JEREMIAH 17.7–8, 14 *Heal me, O Lord*

Blessed are those who trust in the Lord, whose trust is the Lord.
They shall be like a tree planted by water, sending out its roots by the stream.
It shall not fear when heat comes, and its leaves shall stay green;
in the year of drought it is not anxious, and it does not cease to bear fruit.
Heal me, O Lord, and I shall be healed; save me, and I shall be saved;
for you are my praise.

LAMENTATIONS 3.19–24 *The steadfast love of the Lord*

The thought of my affliction and my homelessness is wormwood and gall!
My soul continually thinks of it and is bowed down within me.
But this I call to mind, and therefore I have hope:
The steadfast love of the Lord never ceases,
his mercies never come to an end;
they are new every morning;
great is your faithfulness.
'The Lord is my portion,' says my soul, 'therefore I will hope in him.'

2 KINGS 20.1–5 *Hezekiah's Illness*

In those days Hezekiah became sick and was at the point of death. The prophet Isaiah son of Amoz came to him, and said to him, 'Thus says the Lord: Set your house in order, for you shall die; you shall not recover.' Then Hezekiah turned his face to the wall and prayed to the Lord: 'Remember now, O Lord, I implore you, how I have walked before you in faithfulness with a whole heart, and have done what is good in your sight.' Hezekiah wept bitterly. Before Isaiah had gone out of the middle court, the word of the Lord came to him: 'Turn back, and say to Hezekiah prince of my people, Thus says the Lord, the God of your ancestor David: I have heard your prayer, I have seen your tears; indeed, I will heal you; on the third day you shall go up to the house of the Lord.'

The man (whose appearance was like bronze) brought me back to the entrance of the temple; there, water was flowing from below the threshold of the temple towards the east (for the temple faced east); and the water was flowing down from below the south end of the threshold of the temple, south of the altar. Then he brought me out by way of the north gate, and led me round on the outside to the outer gate that faces towards the east; and the water was coming out on the south side. Going on eastwards with a cord in his hand, the man measured one thousand cubits, and then led me through the water; and it was ankle-deep. Again he measured one thousand, and led me through the water; and it was knee-deep. Again he measured one thousand, and led me through the water; and it was up to the waist. Again he measured one thousand, and it was a river that I could not cross, for the water had risen; it was deep enough to swim in, a river that could not be crossed. He said to me, 'Mortal, have you seen this?' Then he led me back along the bank of the river. As I came back, I saw on the bank of the river a great many trees on one side and on the other. He said to me, 'This water flows towards the eastern region and goes down into the Arabah; and when it enters the sea, the sea of stagnant waters, the water will become fresh. Wherever the river goes, every living creature that swarms will live, and there will be very many fish, once these waters reach there. It will become fresh; and everything will live where the river goes. People will stand fishing beside the sea from En-gedi to En-eglaim; it will be a place for the spreading of nets; its fish will be of a great many kinds, like the fish of the Great Sea. But its swamps and marshes will not become fresh; they are to be left for salt. On the banks, on both sides of the river, there will grow all kinds of trees for food. Their leaves will not wither nor their fruit fail, but they will bear fresh fruit every month, because the water for them flows from the sanctuary. Their fruit will be for food, and their leaves for healing.'

PSALMS

PSALM 23.1–6 *The Lord is my shepherd*

The Lord is my shepherd;
therefore can I lack nothing.
He makes me lie down in green pastures
and leads me beside still waters.
He shall refresh my soul
and guide me in the paths of righteousness for his name's sake.
Though I walk through the valley of the shadow of death,
I will fear no evil;
for you are with me;
your rod and your staff, they comfort me.
You spread a table before me
in the presence of those who trouble me;
you have anointed my head with oil
and my cup shall be full.
Surely goodness and loving mercy shall follow me
all the days of my life,
and I will dwell in the house of the Lord for ever.

PSALM 27.1–5 *The Lord is my light and my salvation*

The Lord is my light and my salvation;
whom then shall I fear?
The Lord is the strength of my life;
of whom then shall I be afraid?
When the wicked, even my enemies and my foes
came upon me to eat up my flesh,
they stumbled and fell.
Though a host encamp against me
my heart shall not be afraid,
and though there rise up war against me,
yet will I put my trust in him.
One thing have I asked of the Lord
and that alone I seek:
that I may dwell in the house of the Lord
all the days of my life.
To behold the fair beauty of the Lord

and to seek his will in his temple.
For in the day of trouble;
he shall hide me in his shelter;
in the secret place of his dwelling shall he hide me
and set me high upon a rock.

PSALM 46.1–7 *God is our refuge and strength*

God is our refuge and strength,
a very present help in trouble.
Therefore we will not fear, though the earth be moved,
and though the mountains tremble in the heart of the sea.
Though the waters rage and swell,
and though the mountains quake at the towering seas.
There is a river whose streams make glad the city of God,
the holy place of the dwelling of the Most High.
God is in the midst of her;
therefore shall she not be removed;
God shall help her at the break of day.
The nations are in uproar and the kingdoms are shaken
but God utters his voice and the earth shall melt away.
The Lord of hosts is with us;
the God of Jacob is our stronghold.

PSALM 91.14–16 *Those who love me I will deliver*

Because they have set their love upon me,
therefore will I deliver them;
I will lift them up, because they know my name.
They will call upon me and I will answer them;
I am with them in trouble,
I will deliver them and bring them to honour.
With long life will I satisfy them
and show them my salvation.

PSALM 103.1–5 *Bless the Lord, O my soul*

Bless the Lord, O my soul,
and all that is within me, bless his holy name.

Bless the Lord, O my soul,
and forget not all his benefits –
who forgives all your sins
and heals all your infirmities;
who redeems your life from the Pit,
who crowns you with faithful love and compassion;
who satisfies you with good things,
so that your youth is renewed like the eagle's.

PSALM 145.136–21 *The Lord watches over all who love him*

The Lord is sure in all his words
and faithful in all his deeds.
The Lord upholds all those who
and lifts up all those who are bowed down.
The eyes of all wait upon you, O Lord,
and you give them their food in due season.
You open wide your hand and fill all things living with plenty.
The Lord is righteous in all his ways
and loving in all his works.
The Lord is near to those who call on him,
to all who call upon him faithfully.
He fulfils the desire of those who fear him;
he hears their cry and saves them.
The Lord watches over those who love him,
but all the wicked he will destroy.
My mouth shall speak the praise of the Lord,
and let all flesh bless his holy name for ever and ever.

New Testament

ACTS 3.1–10 *The healing of the lame man*

One day Peter and John were going up to the temple at the hour of prayer, at three o'clock in the afternoon. And a man lame from birth was being carried in. People would lay him daily at the gate of the temple called the Beautiful Gate so that he could ask for alms from those entering the temple. When he saw Peter and John about to go into the temple, he asked them for alms. Peter looked intently at him, as did John, and said, 'Look at us.' And he fixed his attention on them, expecting to receive something from them. But Peter said, 'I have no silver or gold, but what I have I give you; in the name of Jesus Christ of Nazareth, stand up and walk.' And he took him by the right hand and raised him up; and immediately his feet and ankles were made strong. Jumping up, he stood and began to walk, and he entered the temple with them, walking and leaping and praising God. All the people saw him walking and praising God, and they recognized him as the one who used to sit and ask for alms at the Beautiful Gate of the temple; and they were filled with wonder and amazement at what had happened to him.

ACTS 9.10–19a *Ananias heals Paul's blindness*

There was a disciple in Damascus named Ananias. The Lord said to him in a vision, 'Ananias.' He answered, 'Here I am, Lord.' The Lord said to him, 'Get up and go to the street called Straight, and at the house of Judas look for a man of Tarsus named Saul. At this moment he is praying, and he has seen in a vision a man named Ananias come in and lay his hands on him so that he might regain his sight.' But Ananias answered, 'Lord, I have heard from many about this man, how much evil he has done to your saints in Jerusalem; and here he has authority from the chief priests to bind all who invoke your name.' But the Lord said to him, 'Go, for he is an instrument whom I have chosen to bring my name before Gentiles and kings and before the people of Israel; I myself will show him how much he must suffer for the sake of my name.' So Ananias went and entered the house. He laid his hands on Saul and said, 'Brother Saul, the Lord Jesus, who appeared to you on your way here, has sent me so that you may regain your sight and be filled with the Holy Spirit.' And immediately something like scales fell from his eyes, and his sight was restored. Then he got up and was baptized, and after taking some food, he regained his strength.

ACTS 19.8–12 *Paul in Ephesus*

Paul entered the synagogue and for three months spoke out boldly, and argued persuasively about the kingdom of God. When some stubbornly refused to believe and spoke evil of the Way before the congregation, he left them, taking the disciples with him, and argued daily in the lecture hall of Tyrannus. This continued for two years, so that all the residents of Asia, both Jews and Greeks, heard the word of the Lord. God did extraordinary miracles through Paul, so that when the handkerchiefs or aprons that had touched his skin were brought to the sick, their diseases left them, and the evil spirits came out of them.

1 CORINTHIANS 12.4–12 *The gifts of the Spirit*

There are varieties of gifts, but the same Spirit; and there are varieties of services, but the same Lord; and there are varieties of activities, but it is the same God who activates all of them in everyone. To each is given the manifestation of the Spirit for the common good. To one is given through the Spirit the utterance of wisdom, and to another the utterance of knowledge according to the same Spirit, to another faith by the same Spirit, to another gifts of healing by the one Spirit, to another the working of miracles, to another prophecy, to another the discernment of spirits, to another various kinds of tongues, to another the interpretation of tongues. All these are activated by one and the same Spirit, who allots to each one individually just as the Spirit chooses. For just as the body is one and has many members, and all the members of the body, though many, are one body, so it is with Christ.

PHILIPPIANS 1.3–11 *I thank my God every time I remember you*

I thank my God every time I remember you, constantly praying with joy in every one of my prayers for all of you, because of your sharing in the gospel from the first day until now. I am confident of this, that the one who began a good work among you will bring it to completion by the day of Jesus Christ. It is right for me to think this way about all of you, because you hold me in your heart, for all of you share in God's grace with me, both in my imprisonment and in the defence and confirmation of the gospel. For God is my witness, how I long for all of you with the compassion of Christ Jesus. And this is my prayer, that your love may overflow more and more with knowledge and full insight to help you to determine what is best, so that on the day of

Christ you may be pure and blameless, having produced the harvest of righteousness that comes through Jesus Christ for the glory and praise of God.

JAMES 5.13–16 *Call for the elders of the Church*

Are any among you suffering? They should pray. Are any cheerful? They should sing songs of praise. Are any among you sick? They should call for the elders of the church and have them pray over them, anointing them with oil in the name of the Lord. The prayer of faith will save the sick, and the Lord will raise them up; and anyone who has committed sins will be forgiven. Therefore confess your sins to one another, and pray for one another, so that you may be healed. The prayer of the righteous is powerful and effective.

ACTS 10.36–43 *Peter in the house of Cornelius*

Peter said, 'You know the message he sent to the people of Israel, preaching peace by Jesus Christ – he is Lord of all. That message spread throughout Judea, beginning in Galilee after the baptism that John announced: how God anointed Jesus of Nazareth with the Holy Spirit and with power; how he went about doing good and healing all who were oppressed by the devil, for God was with him. We are witnesses to all that he did both in Judea and in Jerusalem. They put him to death by hanging him on a tree; but God raised him on the third day and allowed him to appear, not to all the people but to us who were chosen by God as witnesses, and who ate and drank with him after he rose from the dead. He commanded us to preach to the people and to testify that he is the one ordained by God as judge of the living and the dead. All the prophets testify about him that everyone who believes in him receives forgiveness of sins through his name.'

ROMANS 8.13–23 *The sufferings of this present time*

If you live according to the flesh, you will die; but if by the Spirit you put to death the deeds of the body, you will live. For all who are led by the Spirit of God are children of God. For you did not receive a spirit of slavery to fall back into fear, but you have received a spirit of adoption. When we cry, 'Abba! Father!' it is that very Spirit bearing witness with our spirit that we are children of God, and if children, then heirs, heirs of God and joint heirs with Christ – if, in fact, we suffer with him so that we may also be glorified with him. I consider that the sufferings of this present time are not worth comparing with the glory about to be revealed to us. For the creation waits with eager longing for the revealing of the children of God; for the creation was subjected to futility, not of its own will but by the will of the one who subjected it, in hope that the creation itself will be set free from its bondage to decay and will obtain the freedom of the glory of the children of God. We know that the whole creation has been groaning in labour pains until now; and not only the creation, but we ourselves, who have the first fruits of the Spirit, groan inwardly while we wait for adoption, the redemption of our bodies.

2 CORINTHIANS 12.7b–10 *Paul's thorn in the flesh*

To keep me from being too elated, a thorn was given to me in the flesh, a messenger of Satan to torment me, to keep me from being too elated. Three times I appealed to the Lord about this, that it would leave me, but he said to me, 'My grace is sufficient for you, for power is made perfect in weakness.' So, I will boast all the more gladly of my weaknesses, so that the power of Christ may dwell in me. Therefore I am content with weaknesses, insults, hardships, persecutions, and calamities for the sake of Christ; for whenever I am weak, then I am strong.

COLOSSIANS 3.14–17 *Clothe yourselves with love*

Above all, clothe yourselves with love, which binds everything together in perfect harmony. And let the peace of Christ rule in your hearts, to which indeed you were called in the one body. And be thankful. Let the word of Christ dwell in you richly; teach and admonish one another in all wisdom; and with gratitude in your hearts sing psalms, hymns, and spiritual songs to God. And whatever you do, in word or deed, do everything in the name of the Lord Jesus, giving thanks to God the Father through him.

GOSPEL

MARK 1.30–31 *Peter's mother-in-law*

Simon's mother-in-law was in bed with a fever, and they told Jesus about her at once. He came and took her by the hand and lifted her up. Then the fever left her, and she began to serve them.

MATTHEW 9.2–8 *The paralysed man*

Some people were carrying a paralysed man lying on a bed. When Jesus saw their faith, he said to the paralytic, 'Take heart, son; your sins are forgiven.' Then some of the scribes said to themselves, 'This man is blaspheming.' But Jesus, perceiving their thoughts, said, 'Why do you think evil in your hearts? For which is easier, to say, "Your sins are forgiven", or to say, "Stand up and walk"? But so that you may know that the Son of Man has authority on earth to forgive sins' – he then said to the paralytic – 'Stand up, take your bed and go to your home.' And he stood up and went to his home. When the crowds saw it, they were filled with awe, and they glorified God, who had given such authority to human beings.

LUKE 4.16–21 *The Spirit of the Lord is upon me*

When Jesus came to Nazareth, where he had been brought up, he went to the synagogue on the sabbath day, as was his custom. He stood up to read, and the scroll of the prophet Isaiah was given to him. He unrolled the scroll and found the place where it was written: 'The Spirit of the Lord is upon me, because he has anointed me to bring good news to the poor. He has sent me to proclaim release to the captives and recovery of sight to the blind, to let the oppressed go free, to proclaim the year of the Lord's favour.' And he rolled up the scroll, gave it back to the attendant, and sat down. The eyes of all in the synagogue were fixed on him. Then he began to say to them, 'Today this scripture has been fulfilled in your hearing.'

LUKE 7.1–10 *The centurion's servant*

Jesus entered Capernaum. A centurion there had a slave whom he valued highly, and who was ill and close to death. When he heard about Jesus, he sent some Jewish elders to him, asking him to come and heal his slave. When they came to Jesus, they appealed to him earnestly, saying, 'He is worthy of having you do this for him, for he loves our people, and it is he who built our synagogue for us.' And Jesus went with them, but when he was not far from the house, the centurion sent friends to say to him, 'Lord, do not trouble yourself, for I am not worthy to have you come under my roof; therefore I did not presume to come to you. But only speak the word, and let my servant be healed. For I also am a man set under authority, with soldiers under me; and I say to one, "Go," and he goes, and to another, "Come," and he comes, and to my slave, "Do this," and the slave does it.' When Jesus heard this he was amazed at him, and turning to the crowd that followed him, he said, 'I tell you, not even in Israel have I found such faith.' When those who had been sent returned to the house, they found the slave in good health.

LUKE 8.43–48 *The woman with the flow of blood*

There was a woman who had been suffering from haemorrhages for twelve years; and though she had spent all she had on physicians, no one could cure her. She came up behind Jesus and touched the fringe of his clothes, and immediately her haemorrhage stopped. Then Jesus asked, 'Who touched me?' When all denied it, Peter said, 'Master, the crowds surround you and press in on you.' But Jesus said, 'Someone touched me; for I noticed that power had gone out from me.' When the woman saw that she could not remain hidden, she came trembling; and falling down before him, she declared in the presence of all the people why she had touched him, and how she had been immediately healed. He said to her, 'Daughter, your faith has made you well; go in peace.'

LUKE 14.1–6 *The man with dropsy*

On one occasion when Jesus was going to the house of a leader of the Pharisees to eat a meal on the sabbath, they were watching him closely. Just then, in front of him, there was a man who had dropsy.

And Jesus asked the lawyers and Pharisees, 'Is it lawful to cure people on the sabbath, or not?' But they were silent. So Jesus took him and healed him, and sent him away. Then he said to them, 'If one of you has a child or an ox that has fallen into a well, will you not immediately pull it out on a sabbath day?' And they could not reply to this.

LUKE 17.11–19 *The ten lepers*

On the way to Jerusalem Jesus was going through the region between Samaria and Galilee. As he entered a village, ten lepers approached him. Keeping their distance, they called out, saying, 'Jesus, Master, have mercy on us!' When he saw them, he said to them, 'Go and show yourselves to the priests.' And as they went, they were made clean. Then one of them, when he saw that he was healed, turned back, praising God with a loud voice. He prostrated himself at Jesus' feet and thanked him. And he was a Samaritan. Then Jesus asked, 'Were not ten made clean? But the other nine, where are they? Was none of them found to return and give praise to God except this foreigner?' Then he said to him, 'Get up and go on your way; your faith has made you well.'

JOHN 9.1–11 *The blind man*

As Jesus walked along, he saw a man blind from birth. His disciples asked him, 'Rabbi, who sinned, this man or his parents, that he was born blind?' Jesus answered, 'Neither this man nor his parents sinned; he was born blind so that God's works might be revealed in him. We must work the works of him who sent me while it is day; night is coming when no one can work. As long as I am in the world, I am the light of the world.' When he had said this, he spat on the ground and made mud with the saliva and spread the mud on the man's eyes, saying to him, 'Go, wash in the pool of Siloam' (which means Sent). Then he went and washed and came back able to see. The neighbours and those who had seen him before as a beggar began to ask, 'Is this not the man who used to sit and beg?' Some were saying, 'It is he.' Others were saying, 'No, but it is someone like him.' He kept saying, 'I am the man.' But they kept asking him, 'Then how were your eyes opened?' He answered, 'The man called Jesus made mud, spread it on my eyes, and said to me, "Go to Siloam and wash." Then I went and washed and received my sight.'

READINGS

Although the Scriptures are the primary source for reflecting on God's Word – corporately as well as individually – we can still learn much from others' thoughts and experiences of prayer. In this chapter I have assembled a collection of quotations from those who were writing on various aspects of Christian spirituality in the twentieth century. The only reason for my choices is that some of the things these authors have written encouraged me in my spiritual pilgrimage, and I hope these 'tasters' might encourage others as well. Like the Scripture passages in the previous chapter, they have the common themes of being healed, restored and forgiven.

At the end of the day, no human mind can encompass God. Spirituality is in principle a never-ending journey in which new heights and depths are always still to be discovered. Human perfection lies in limitation. Wholeness involves the acceptance of limits, for we are all limited in one way or another.

A Time to Heal

I have to ask forgiveness for many things. I suppose it is wrong to say one is glad to need it, and yet I must confess to that very creaturely feeling, and if I ever honestly had the chance of forgiving some one something very real, it would be, I feel sure, a very high kind of happiness. I am sure forgiving is one of God's greatest joys.

The Life and Letters of Father Andrew[13]

To receive grace is to relate to Jesus and to relate to Jesus can only mean to follow him on the way that leads to the cross. The costliness of that relationship, far from detracting from its graciousness, enhances it, because for Christians the way of the cross is a way that leads to the new life of the resurrection, and closeness to Christ can be at its most real and most intimate when he and we are sharers in suffering. He is indeed with us when we are led by green pastures and still waters, but there is a new dimension to our relationship with him when we walk through the valley of the shadow of death and discover that his rod and his staff, his attentive, protecting companionship comfort us there when most other forms of comfort are gone.

Tom Smail, Windows on the Cross[14]

We pray for the removal of pain, pray passionately and then with exhaustion, sick from hope deferred and prayer's failure. But there is a higher prayer than that. It is a greater thing to pray for pain's conversion than for its removal. It is more of grace to pray that God would make a sacrament of it. The sacrament of pain! That sacrament we partake not simply, nor perhaps chiefly, when we say, or try to say, with resignation, 'Thy will be done.' It is not always easy for the sufferer, if he remains clear-eyed, to see that it is God's will. It may have been caused by an evil mind, or by a light fool, or some stupid greed. But, now it is there, a certain treatment of it is God's will; and that is to capture and exploit it for Him. It is to make it serve the soul and glorify God. It is to consecrate its elements and make it sacramental. It is to convert it into prayer.

P. T. Forsyth, The Soul of Prayer[15]

We can welcome the Cross as a way of experiencing the kind of suffering our Lord experienced. We talk glibly about the Passion and sufferings of our Lord, in a general kind of way without pausing to imagine what they were like. I think often of the disappointment and sadness of our Lord when, early in his ministry, his own kinsmen, his own friends at Nazareth, wanted to throw him down from the cliff. Let us reflect on his being rejected by his own people, deserted by his friends; the dereliction of the garden, the abandonment on the Cross – apart from the physical torment. And yet we learn the secret of the Resurrection when we learn the secret of the Cross. And it is when we are called to share in some way in the suffering of Christ, that we come to understand not only what he experienced but also what this was leading to. For every cross leads to resurrection. I like to think of life as each day being prepared by God's providence, and it is in many ways the road to the Cross. But it leads to a greater understanding of our Lord, a greater sharing in his Resurrection.

Basil Hume, *Searching for God*[16]

In the psalms I am at my worst and my best. Here I can acclaim God with warmth and confidence and hope, but here also I can give vent to those black thoughts that might otherwise lie hidden in the dark and angry corners of my heart. Above all the psalms express the reality of my longing for God and my joy and suffering in the vicissitudes of my search for him. Sometimes God is close, sometimes distant. I seek him in the desert and on the mountain, in poverty and emptiness and in waiting. Today God is mindful of me, tomorrow he may not visit me. Today I am brought to the mountain top, tomorrow I am calling from the depths. Today I am radiant, tomorrow I face darkness. Today I enjoy life, tomorrow I feel the hand of death.

Esther de Waal, *Seeking God: The Way of St Benedict*[17]

What shall I do during prayer? (How eagerly people long to be told the answer! For that would make me safe against God, well protected: I would know what to do!) But the answer is of the usual appalling simplicity: stand before God unprotected, and you will know yourself what to do. I mean this in utter earnest. Methods are of value, naturally, but only as something to do 'if I want to', which in this context of response to God means: if he wants me to. I may feel drawn to meditate, to sing to him, to stay before him in, say, an attitude of contrition or praise; most often I shall probably want to do nothing but be in his presence. Whether I am aware of that presence does not matter. I know he is there, whatever my feelings, just as Jesus knew when he felt abandoned on the cross. What pure praise of the Father's love; to feel abandoned and yet stay content before him, saying, 'Father, into your hands . . .' We cannot sufficiently emphasise to ourselves that prayer is God's concern, and his one desire is 'to come and make his abode with us.'

Wendy Beckett, *The Mystery of Love*[18]

The growth in moral and spiritual freedom which Christ enables is no smooth and easy progress. It is punctuated by crises in which we are made to feel our weakness and vulnerability. For we grow in freedom step by step without growth in reliance upon God. The trials and temptations which bring home to us our liability to slip and full force us to turn to Christ our Helper and Deliverer as our only hope. 'When I am weak,' St Paul writes, 'then I am strong' (2 Cor. 12.10). The paradox is explained in the fact that the feeling of weakness compels us to rely on the inexhaustible strength of God. It is well to bear this in mind and so forestall discouragement when trouble comes. Those strongly committed to the spiritual journey are often disconcerted by the recurrence of old temptations which they believed they had conquered long ago. We may find ourselves haunted by doubting or blasphemous thoughts, by feelings of anger, hate or depression, by lust or by dark suspicions about others. Once perhaps we were able to dismiss these unwelcome visitors by an effort of will, now we may have to learn to rely on the grace of Christ; we progress not by trying harder, but by trusting more. This type of experience is part of our sharing the vulnerability of Christ. Out of the crucible of temptation we emerge into a new freedom and an altogether deeper reliance on God.

Christopher Bryant, *Journey to the Centre*[19]

The sacramental act of anointing is supremely a community event. There will be times when someone is visiting a friend who is sick and it is entirely appropriate to offer prayer for healing for that person. . . But alongside this spontaneous ministry there needs to be the corporate acts of faith such as the anointing with oil by the elders. It is my belief that when we engage in these corporate acts, the spiritual health of the corporate groups will have some influence. God has always called his people to dwell in community, whether it be the people of Israel in the Old Covenant or the Body of Christ in the New. The so-called 'high priestly' prayer of Jesus in John 17 ('that they may be one') suggests that Jesus knew how hard it was going to be for us to achieve good levels of unity. The history of the Church over the past two thousand years, and a casual glance at churches today, suggest that we have a long way to go to achieve the kind of love for one another that Jesus prayed, and prays for. One of the reasons why we need to love one another is to develop the kind of community in which will flow the healing love of God. Can we really with all integrity hold a healing service for the sick when we are fighting each other in church council meetings? Simplistic though it may sound, the more love there is in a church, the more likely there is to be healing.

Michael Mitton, *Wild Beasts and Angels*[20]

Jesus broke the bread of the Supper into as many pieces as there were disciples present. Peter took one piece, John another and soon there was none of it remaining. He gave his mysterious body away to his friends without remainder and without reserve, for that was the principle of his life. He also said to his disciples, 'Give, and it shall be given unto you.' But I do not find that I give myself away as he gave himself away. I find that I am jealously keeping my life for myself, stealing this and that part from my neighbour and from God, making up little closed packets of pleasure and pride. 'Give, and it shall be given unto you.' If we could once for all give ourselves away, be perfectly at the disposal of God and of men, Jesus would fully give himself to us.

Austin Farrer, *The Crown of the Year*[21]

Every now and then our eyes are opened and we see beyond the narrowness of our day-to-day vision. This was expressed by Jacob when he awoke out of sleep, a sleep he felt he had been in all his life up to that point: 'Jacob awoke out of sleep and said, "Surely, the Lord is in this place, and I knew it not." And he was afraid and said, "How aweful is this place! This is none other than the house of God, and this is the gate of heaven"' (Genesis 28.16–17). Jacob had not been looking for this experience, it had suddenly opened before him. I believe that such experiences are offered to all of us at one time or another in our lives. But we in our turn have to be open enough to receive them. Such vistas often come before us at a point of crisis in our lives, when we are suddenly bereaved, or made redundant, or when we are having what the world calls a breakdown. Often we become more aware because we have become dislocated, just as we are more aware of a limb that has been dislocated. If we face the unfamiliar it may open all sorts of gates for us. Prayer is not an escape from such situations but an entering deeper into the reality of what is going on around us. Prayer should help us to extend ourselves and our lives. Prayer will not rescue us from the situation, but it should help us to see it more clearly, and to recognize that we are not alone in it.

David Adam, *The Open Gate*[22]

Let us, by an act of will, place ourselves in the presence of our Divine Lord and, with an act of faith, ask that He will empty us of self and of ALL desire save that His most blessed will may be done, and that it may illumine our hearts and minds. We can then gather together all those for whom our prayers have been asked, and hold them silently up to Him, making no special request – neither asking nor beseeching – but just resting with them, IN Him, desiring nothing but that Our Lord may be glorified in them . . . In this most simple way of approach He does make known His Most Blessed Will for us.

Dorothy Kerin, *The Burrswood Healing Service*[23]

Compassion is only another name for love. And love is caring, caring with the deep care of God. . . Love is an affair, not primarily of the emotions but of the will, so that we can love someone whom we do not naturally like. And it is directed at the other person's eternal welfare. So it may well correspond with the description of a Northern saint which ran like this: 'He was strangely austere, strangely tender; strangely gentle, strangely inflexible.' For this compassionate living, thank God, there are divine resources available. 'The love of God has been shed in our hearts by the Holy Spirit given to us' (Romans 55). The phrase, 'shed abroad,' is the same as that used in Joel 2.28 of the pouring out of the Holy Spirit on God's servants. Thus God's compassion comes through the Christian to meet and succour those who are in need, in loneliness, in distress. Thus gradually and bit by bit the marks of St Paul's great hymn to love, given to us in 1 Corinthians 13, are seen in us, and we become a blessing to others.

Donald Coggan, *Christian Priorities*[24]

SOURCES AND ACKNOWLEDGEMENTS

I am grateful to my wife, Margaret, and to Christine Burry for valuable help in composing the prayer on pp. 28–29. The prayers in the section on 'The Ministry of Reconciliation' on pp. 85f. have been compiled from Anglican sources. The sources of other prayers and services are listed below.

1 *A Time to Heal*, Church House Publishing, 2000. Quotations are taken from pp. 14, 296, 274, 298, 316, 254, 233, 144, 122, xiii, 18 and 144.
2 *New Patterns for Worship*, Church House Publishing, 2002, F22, p. 86.
3 *Common Worship: Pastoral Services*, Church House Publishing, 2000, p. 92, copyright © The Archbishops' Council 2000 and used by permission.
4 *Common Worship: Pastoral Services*, p. 31.
5 *Common Worship: Pastoral Services*, pp. 14f.
6 *Common Worship: Pastoral Services* and *Common Worship: Services and Prayers for the Church of England*, Church House Publishing 2000, copyright © The Archbishops' Council 2000 and used by permission.
7 *Lent, Holy Week, Easter*, Church House Publishing, 1986, p. 56.
8 The Retired Clergy Association of the Church of England, slightly adapted.
9 Desmond O'Donnell and Maureen Mohen, *Praying the Good News*, Fount, 1998, printed with the permission of the authors.
10 George Appleton, *One Man's Prayers*, SPCK, 1977, printed with the permission of the publishers.
11 Christopher and Josephine Bunch, *Prayers for Everyday Use*, Canterbury Press 1992, p.35, printed with the permission of the publishers.
12 Percy Dearmer, *The Parson's Handbook*, 1907. Dearmer was vicar of St Mary's, Primrose Hill, London, in the early years of the last century. He did much to encourage the revival of the healing ministry in the Church of England. These two prayers appeared in a form of service for anointing with the laying on of hands.
13 Kathleen E. Burne (ed.), *The Life and Letters of Father Andrew*, SDC, Mowbray, 1948, p. 255.
14 Tom Smail, *Windows on the Cross*, Darton, Longman & Todd, 1995, p. 96, printed with author's permission.
15 P. T. Forsyth, *The Soul of Prayer*, Epworth Press, n.d., pp. 58–59.
16 Basil Hume, OSB, *Searching for God*, Hodder & Stoughton, 1977, pp. 143–44.
17 Esther de Waal, *Seeking God: The Way of St Benedict,* Collins Fount Paperbacks, 1984, p. 149, printed with the author's permission.

18 Sister Wendy Beckett, *The Mystery of Love*, HarperCollins, 1996, p. x.
19 Christopher Bryant, *Journey to the Centre*, Darton, Longman & Todd, 1987, p. 55, printed with the permission of the Society of St John the Evangelist.
20 Michael Mitton, *Wild Beasts and Angels*, Darton, Longman & Todd, 2000, pp. 107–8.
21 Austin Farrer, *The Crown of the Year*, Dacre Press: A. & C. Black, 1952, p. 51.
22 David Adam, *The Open Gate*, SPCK, Triangle, 1994, pp. 2–3.
23 Dorothy Kerin, *The Burrswood Healing Service*, quoted by Johanna Ernest in *The Life of Dorothy Kerin*, Dorothy Kerin Trust, 1983.
24 Donald Coggan, *Christian Priorities*, Lutterworth Press, 1963, p. 80.